GARDEN
BOUNDARIES

GARDEN
BOUNDARIES

20 projects for

trellises walls fences gates screens hedges

TOBY BUCKLAND

LAUREL
GLEN

San Diego, California

contents

planning a garden landscape

your GARDEN BOUNDARY

The concept of boundaries doesn't immediately appear to be a particularly inspiring one in the realm of garden design, but imagine how it feels to sit outside in your garden, enclosed by light-filtering trellis entwined with clematis and fragrant roses. Suddenly it takes on a whole new meaning. The right hedge, fence, or wall can enhance your garden, making it a comfortable and beautiful place to be.

A combination of ground cover and hedges entices you to explore.

The importance of boundaries

Boundaries are the key feature of a well-designed garden. They enclose its sides, separate one part from another, and define its focal points and views. Their influence is far-reaching—boundaries touch all aspects of gardening, from where the sunshine or shadows fall, to the position of entrances. They even define a garden's atmosphere and how it feels. The right boundary enhances a garden, whereas a poor one detracts from it like peeling paint or broken steps.

I recently bought a new house, and a bigger piece of land was definitely one of the main selling points. Stepping out into the new garden was like walking across a giant blank canvas; it was full of potential but largely empty. Out the back door, across the patio, the lawn stretched to a perimeter of hedges and fences—all of which I owned, and all of which were overgrown or falling apart. Although far from the house, this motley mix of wood and foliage was the most magnetic part of the garden, drawing the eye and making the whole place appear unkempt.

One year later, the picture is very different. At the back of the garden, the old hedge remains, but in front of it a living wall made of willow meanders around. Last spring, I ordered willow branches from a local nursery—twenty bundles of red and pea-green willow whips. After a day of cutting, weaving, and piling in topsoil, the branches had been turned into a living willow wall, blurring the boundary of the garden with the countryside beyond and demarcating the space for a new small orchard. In a space of just eight yards, the whole feel and function of the garden had been transformed.

That's just one change; there have been many others—a cypress hedge was exchanged for a privacy fence; tumbling slopes were retained with railroad ties and bricks; countless details were added to smaller parts of the garden, making these areas more private, luxurious places to sit. One of my favorite new details is the copper-clad wall—originally, the wall was just plastered concrete blocks shaped into an arch, but with the addition of a piece of copper that was cut to size and magically aged, it is now an abstract picture painted in cobalt blue.

More than simply adding detail, the new boundaries have broken up the garden, engendered the whole place with a sense of mystery, and given each individual area a purpose. Now when you step out of the back door, paths between low hedges and walls entice you to explore the orchard, the cut flowers, and the tropical garden—each with its own ambience and theme. At the same time, subtle gates through internal divides tempt you into secret areas that lie unnoticed until you happen upon them.

Using this book

This book is a practical guide for making your own unique garden boundaries, both around the perimeter of your garden and for dividing it into smaller areas. You'll find advice on building all kinds of walls, fences, and screens, plus information on planting and customizing living boundaries. In addition to step-by-step projects and chapters explaining the essential tools, techniques, and suppliers, this book is packed with original, inspirational photography to help you visualize how boundaries could work in your own garden.

The inclusion of an arch and a wrought iron gate adds a magical touch to this beech hedge.

Consider how your boundary can also serve seating or lighting purposes.

Boundaries explained

Boundaries have two major functions: physically stopping you in your tracks and/or blocking your view or your neighbor's. Most perimeter boundaries form a physical barrier, but that doesn't necessarily mean that they obscure the view of a garden. Indeed, in front yards, the boundary is often low and exists simply to mark a change in property ownership and to discourage trespassers.

Visual boundaries (those that block your view) needn't be solid and can be achieved by planting a bushy evergreen in front of a view. You can walk around the evergreen, but from behind its foliage, you can't see out and no one can see in.

Design

Applying garden design to boundaries is primarily about deciding on the best place for screens, where to place entrances through external divides, and whether views should be blocked or framed. The trick to good garden design isn't just getting things in the right place; it's about making them work really hard, so that they not only serve a purpose, but they also have a lot of style. A retaining wall in the right place and with the right coping, for example, can double up as a seating area. Choosing appropriate materials to blend in with chosen themes and style is just as important.

For most people, many of these decisions are quite instinctive, due to our natural understanding of spaces that feel oppressive—and others that feel too exposed. Every garden is different, so decide where you most like sitting in your garden, and make your internal boundaries around these spaces. The same instinct comes into play when deciding where entrances should be sited and how high a hedge or fence should be.

This book was created for inspiration, but it is primarily a manual; use it while you work and don't be afraid to get sawdust and soil between the pages. Good luck!

choosing STYLES

The choice of garden boundaries is huge, although researching through books or on the Internet will give you an idea of which types are historically accurate or appropriate for your home. The decision is often a tug-of-war between personal taste and what your budget and local laws will allow.

Knowing what you like is one thing, but re-creating it in your own garden is another. If you're unsure, go on an "expedition" to check out the boundaries in other people's gardens. It's not enough simply to look—you've got to make a mental note of what works and what doesn't, and ask yourself why. Do the bricks clash with those used in the house? Are the hedges too imposing? Are the fences poorly built or so lacking in detail that they detract from the garden itself? Once you start, you'll notice the good, the bad, and the ugly boundaries on every street; but most importantly, you'll pick up tips and ideas about how to make the ones you like work in your own garden.

Start by thinking about the purpose you want the boundary to serve, and consider the following issues.

Views

Assess whether there are any features, near or far, such as church spires or power lines, that you either want to emphasize or obscure. If a boundary is close to you, it doesn't need to be very high to hide distant eyesores. So, as well as perimeter boundaries, consider using internal screens around seating areas and viewpoints.

Microclimate

Boundaries have a job to do, filtering and enhancing the weather: a stone wall in the right place will hold the heat of the sun well into the evening, while a soil-filled willow wall will always feel cool, benefiting plants that perform best in shady spots. When it comes to buffeting winds, a solid wall is not as effective as one that lets some air through. In fact, a fence with gaps, such as a picket fence or shadow box fence, will slow the wind without creating turbulence as the air swirls over the top.

Security

Small gardens present the biggest problem when creating a secure boundary, because you can't have a high, dominant boundary. But even a low, see-through enclosure will discourage cats and dogs from straying onto your property and will present a visual deterrent. Even a tall boundary will not deter thieves, but it will prevent them from eyeing valuable items in your home, as well as slowing their access.

Vertical gardening

Obviously, walls and fences provide support for climbers and wall shrubs, but identifying your sunny sites will give you the opportunity to grow tender or half-hardy, more unusual plants—not just climbers, but shrubs and perennials that will thrive in the warmth reflected at the base of the

A clean-cut serpentine hedge.

Braided hornbeams form a vertical screen.

support. In addition, tall vertical plants can form a boundary in themselves if trained correctly. Some of the projects in this book offer ways to grow plants not only on the boundary, but also inside it, due to the soil and built-in irrigation within that keeps plants watered. It's a way of elevating the garden, and it's ideal if you have trouble bending over, because it brings the flowers up to waist height.

Intimacy

Boundaries can shield seating areas and patios from the gaze of overlooking windows. For maximum effect, the choice of boundary and its position are essential. Where space is limited and sunlight is at a premium—as with many city gardens—a close, miniboundary along one side of a patio, rather than the whole area, is often all you need to make a seating area private. For this, the best boundaries are frosted glass screens or flower-covered trellises. Larger gardens can be made private by growing hedges and trees behind fences or around gates, or by growing clematis or jasmine to create an extra 2–3 ft. of foliage screening.

Nestle gates in foliage for an intimate feel.

Noise barriers

The thicker the boundary, the greater its ability to deflect noise. Planter walls, dense hedges, or thick wooden railroad ties, combined with dense plantings and foliage, all help to make your space quieter.

Dense foliage creates an effective noise barrier.

Details

Boundaries offer incredible opportunities for detail, from copper cladding to trellises to pretty plantings. By using luxurious or unusual materials, even the smallest areas can be enhanced, leaving ground space free for decorative pots and garden furniture.

Entrances

Enclosures and the entrances through them are inseparable. Indeed, entrances make the focal points for vistas and views, and offer opportunities for pretty detailing. An entrance can say a great deal and depending on the message you want to get across, can be imposing, inviting, prominent, or concealed. The primary function of an entrance is, of course, to provide access, but a gate is a way of giving you that feeling of enclosure in what would normally just be a thoroughfare.

Staggered bamboo screen invites you to enter.

Seating

Boundaries create backdrops, and they can be a perfect place to position a seat. Seats may be designed into the boundary, perhaps in the corner of a fence, under a clipped arch in a hedge, or on top of a low retaining wall made of concrete blocks.

Terracing

Boundaries are a way of retaining soil, transforming sloping gardens into leveled areas that are easier to maintain. They also offer ways of bringing in interest from steps, plinths topped with flowering urns, and cascading water features.

Walls can incorporate shallow steps and plants.

choosing MATERIALS

Once you've decided on the function of your boundary, it's time to choose materials and a suitable style. Provided that different parts of the garden are visually enclosed so that you don't see more than one at a time, you don't need to restrict yourself to just one type of material. Of course, it's best if you can link them in some way by repeating themes.

Treat your house as the most important boundary, dictating not only the flavor of the area around it, but also absorbing some of the character of the garden. Many designers forget that the house can be used to blend with the garden, as much as the garden should blend with the house. For example, a trellis screen could be made more relevant to the area around the patio by attaching some trellises to the house, as well. Or, if you are using copper cladding on a wall (see pages 96–97), repeat the theme with copper-cladded window boxes and sconces.

If you have a new house, the boundary will often be made up of just one type of fencing. Because it is costly to remove the fencing, add details that will make it more interesting instead. For example, you could add finials on top of fence posts, a new layer of paint, or trellis cladding.

Internal boundaries can be treated in the same way, provided they have some link to the house or garden.

Materials

There are dozens of materials for garden boundaries, each with its own personality. Base your choice on how it blends in with your existing materials, themes, and preferred style, as well as price and practicality.

Wood

Wood is extremely versatile and is the easiest material to turn into custom boundaries because it can be cut to any shape. It's also fairly inexpensive. In a garden, its look is warm, and as far as style is concerned, wood is a bit of a chameleon—rustic or modern, left rough-hewn or given a lick of paint, any style can be attractive.

Weathered oak door.

Stone

Natural stone instantly ages a garden and has a feeling of quality. Used with a little imagination, this feeling of antiquity can be enhanced by combining stone with plants. Stone can also be given a fresh, modern look when used with metalwork (see pages 52–53). Local stone is usually the cheapest option, and it often blends well, but in enclosed areas there is no reason why you can't use more colorful stone or paint it with a color of your choice.

Painted plaster.

Metal

Traditionally, metal is used to give a very formal front face to a garden. Ironwork railings and wrought-iron fences are best left to blacksmiths, however, it is possible to use some metals, like sheet copper and wire mesh, in do-it-yourself projects with few tools and minimal knowledge.

The effects that metal creates are fresh, contemporary, and so beautiful that they wouldn't be out of place on the walls of an art gallery. Because

Louvered metal gate.

Living willow fence.

Sandblasted glass screen.

metal is relatively cheap to buy, the look comes without a huge price tag.

Stems

Willow and hazel are easy, quick, and fun to work with, and they allow you to use your imagination. They also require the least preparation of the materials. While they don't last as long as more robust materials, you can

expect three to six years out of them. Living willow has the advantage of rooting, and if kept watered, will last indefinitely. If it gets too big, chop it down in the winter.

Glass

Glass is mostly used for detailing in boundaries—for example, stained glass in trellises. If you're looking for a

contemporary-style screen, sandblasted safety glass makes an ideal internal boundary that allows light to pass through. Combined with architectural plants, safety glass creates interesting silhouettes in sun or nighttime lighting. It is equivalent in price to a good brick wall, but it is quicker to make.

Brick

Brick, with its warm, solid appearance, is the classic boundary material. Its variations are infinite—from the way it is laid to methods of pointing and brick bonds, not to mention the many colors and finishes of the bricks themselves. They do take a certain amount of skill to lay, but with practice, anyone can make a decent low wall. The cost is high, but you can save money when building your own with a few tricks of the trade (see pages 24–25 and 54–55).

A: London multistock reclaimed
B: Handmade soft red
C: Red stock
D: Machine-made Burwell white
E: Tudor Red reclaimed
F: Combination handmade reclaimed
G: New handmade stock
H: Combination multi handmade reclaimed

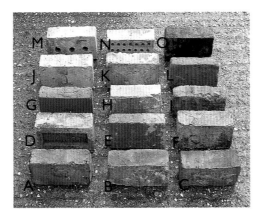

I: Yellow stock
J: Combination machine-made stock
K: Combination multistock machine-made
L: Tudor red
M: Combination machine-made stock
N: Reclaimed pot or perforated
O: Staffs Blue England

order OF WORK

Before starting construction, professional builders and landscapers write out the sequence of events needed to get the job done on a list known as the "order of work." It's not only a time-saver, it also preempts many possible problems in accessing the site, storing materials, and renting equipment.

Planning ahead

• *Stacking materials:* If you intend to build a boundary over a period of a number of months, it won't be appropriate to leave the materials on the lawn. It is much better to organize deliveries for when you need them.

• *Rental equipment:* Whether it's a drill, a cement mixer, or a wheelbarrow, it's important to get them when you have the time to do the work, so order in advance.

• *Delivery dates and times:* Make sure it won't be inconvenient to take time off work. If you won't be home, be sure that you've given exact instructions about where the delivery is to be placed to avoid coming home to find that your driveway is taken up by four tons of sand.

• *Noise:* Always check with neighbors about the best times to have deliveries and to use loud machinery and power tools.

• *Access:* What is the quickest way and least troublesome route from where materials are delivered to where you want to use them? Are there any shortcuts? For example, by temporarily removing a fence panel, can you speed up the process?

• *Timing:* If you're building more than just boundaries (perhaps putting in a path or patio, as well), examine which has the deepest footing. A wall has deeper footings than a path, so it will always be built before putting down paving. Trellises, on the other hand, have a shallower footing, so it's best to put them in afterward to keep access open and avoid damaging what you've just done.

Estimating materials

Once you've decided on your style of boundary, you need to estimate quantities and buy the materials. This is something that all good home-improvement stores will be able to help with, provided you know what materials you want. So, arm yourself with knowledge—shop around, have a

Ballast bag.

look at materials, take a photo of your garden or features to help you match materials, or find pictures from books or magazines that you are trying to duplicate. Visit salvage yards and metalwork shops—places you might not ordinarily go to—for inspiration.

Inevitably, you will have to modify designs from pictures and step-by-step books to fit your location, particularly if you are making a custom project, such as trellises (see pages 88–91). Draw a sketch of your idea or, better yet, a scale drawing, so you can accurately quantify the materials you will need. Scale drawings are done with a scale ruler that shows every 3 ft. represented as $1/2$–4 in., depending on how detailed you want the drawing. Remember that if you are building anything from wood and it involves a lot of cutting to length, add an extra ten percent for waste.

The following are typical quantities for standard boundaries.

Walls

One ton of sand or ballast equals $26^1/_2$ cubic feet in volume. For concrete foundations, you need six and a half 50-lb. bags of cement per ton of ballast. For 3 ft. of single-skin wall, you need sixty bricks (120 for a double-skin wall) plus ten for breakages (see box on page 25 for an explanation of types of walls). For 3 ft. of concrete block wall (using standard 4-in. blocks laid on their sides), you need twenty-one blocks. One ton of sand combined with eight bags of cement is enough to lay approximately 41½ ft. of double-skin walling or 96 ft. of concrete blocks.

Privacy fence

For every linear yard of privacy fence, you need eight 6-in tapered boards.

Tapered boards.

Willow

One standard bundle of willow makes approximately 1½ sq. ft. of willow wall.

Willow wall.

Stone

You get 40 sq. ft. of wall per ton of stone, depending on the type of stone used.

Stone planter wall.

How to buy

If you have previously concentrated on small-scale garden jobs, you're probably accustomed to buying materials in small bags and taking them home in your car. For larger jobs, you'll have to get materials delivered to your home, and depending on the material in question, this can have cost implications.

Buying stone, gravel, sand, and ballast

Stone, gravel, sand, and ballast are all cheapest to buy when delivered loose, but that leaves you with the problem of storage and cleaning up. For instance, builder's sand will stain a driveway, so it must be contained on plastic sheeting. Slightly more expensive but far more convenient are large, white ballast bags or pallets. This is definitely the best option if the job is going to take a while, because it keeps out cats and water and looks much neater.

Buying bricks.

Buying wood

Wood is sold in standard lengths and sizes, depending on the type of wood. This could be 10-ft. and 16-ft. lengths; for example, if your job involves 8-ft. lengths of wood, research the standard sizes before buying to be sure you are not paying for wood that will go to waste. Wood is readily available from home-improvement stores. For older, more interesting wood, check out salvage yards.

Wood is delivered in individual planks, so if there will be a time delay before using it, keep it flat to prevent it from bowing. It is also important to protect it from wetness, or it may twist out of shape.

Buying wood from a salvage yard.

tools and techniques

marking OUT

Marking out is the process of transferring the penciled features on a garden design into lines on the ground and creating reference points. It allows for speedy, accurate construction and gives you one last chance to alter your plans. Be sure to mark out the job carefully, as errors can make the process of building and quantifying problematic.

Making a 3-4-5 triangle

Creating a right angle on paper is easily done, but to transfer such measurements onto the ground you need to do a little math. It's not complicated, though, and getting it right now will make things much easier for you later.

The technique was discovered by the Greek mathematician Pythagoras some 2,500 years ago, and it involves making a triangle on the ground. If the base is 3 ft. long, the side 4 ft., and the diagonal 5 ft., the corner where the base and side connect will be a perfect right angle. The quickest way to mark this is with 12 ft. of measuring tape looped around a triangle of bamboo sticks

Make a 3-4-5 triangle.

pushed into the ground. Hold the ends of the zero and 12-ft. mark of the tape next to one stick and move the other sticks to the 4-ft. and 9-ft. marks to get your right angle.

External boundaries and not offending the neighbors

Disputes over the boundaries between properties are one of the main causes of conflict between neighbors, therefore, it is essential to check deeds of ownership before commencing work on any perimeter boundary. It is also prudent to check with your neighbors first about any changes you are making and to get permission to enter their garden while working on the divide. If you are replacing a fence, always build to the line of the old one and confirm with your neighbors that your string marking lines are in the right place, in order to avoid any disputes.

Marking and fixing fence posts

To mark out the line of a fence, fix the two end fence posts in position and run a taut line between their bases— you may need to tie back any overhanging branches or herbaceous plants that get in the way.

Starting at one end, mark the position of the intermediate fence posts. Depending on the design of the

Mark positions of posts on the ground.

fence, the fence posts will either occur down its center or be on the owner's side, so that the flat face of the fence runs along the boundary.

If any posts coincide with a drain or old concrete hold, digging a hole or hammering in a fence spike will be impossible. Either move all of the post positions along to avoid the obstacle, or if you are building a picket or privacy fence, have a longer rail for that one section.

If you are building a panel fence, moving the position of the fence posts will more than likely mean that the end panels will have to be cut down to fit the run (see pages 26–27).

If the posts are to be concreted in place, dig the holes for all of the intermediate posts, making them 24 in. deep and 6–8 in. wide. Then run another string line between the two end posts at their tops. If the end posts are upright, then when each intermediate fence post is brought up against the top and bottom string line, it will be upright, too. Finally, check that it is level side to side before bracing and concreting in place.

Use a taut line to position the posts.

Scoring an arc using a stake and string

Curved patios and paths, along with the boundaries that flank them, produce an informal look that blends well with planting. Walls that double up as seating benefit from being curved, as they allow people to face each other when seated, and because they are curved, their stability is increased.

You can mark a serpentine or curved line on the ground by eye, but doesn't tend to look natural. A more reliable method is to tie a length of string to a stake pushed in at the center of your arc. Hold the string taut at the point where you want the radius, and use it as a guide as you spray-paint or sprinkle sand along your line.

Score an arc.

Rather than being arbitrary about the position of the curves, arc them around existing features of a garden (trees and seating areas, for example), because this helps to unify and tie the features in a garden together.

Using fence spikes

Fence spikes take away all the hard work of digging holes. After marking out the positions of the posts, use a sledgehammer to drive the fence spikes into the ground. Custom-made, plastic driving units are available that fit onto the spike and take the impact of the hammer, preventing damage to the spikes. These also have metal bars that allow you to knock them back into line if they start to twist.

The trick to getting fence spikes upright is to check with a level after every few blows with the hammer.

If the spikes need straightening, hammer the driver against the direction they lean to bring them upright. Once in the ground, hammer the post into the socket of the fence spike while ensuring that it is firm and upright. The best fence post systems have bolts that let you tighten the metal around the base of the post.

Use a level to check that the spikes are upright.

These allow a little movement, making it easy to make adjustments and get the posts perfectly upright.

Tighten the fence posts into position.

As well as spikes, there are many different metal fence fixings, including sockets for bolting the base of a post to concrete, spikes that drive into the hole left after a rotten fence post has snapped, and sockets for extending the height of your fence. They all work well, but if you use them, aim to disguise all metal spikes and fixings beneath evergreen plantings or below the soil.

concrete,
MORTAR, AND FOUNDATIONS

This section is about the two glues that hold the hard landscaping in a garden together—concrete and mortar. Understanding how to make and use them is an essential part of many do-it-yourself garden projects, including building walls, setting fence posts, laying paving, and making water features.

The ingredients

Concrete and mortar have different applications. Mortar is used to set materials such as bricks and paving stones on a level, while concrete is used for the foundations of walls, paths, and fence posts.

Sharp sand

A washed sand with angular grains that fills the spaces between stones in concrete. Because their sides are angular, the grains lock together, giving concrete its strength. A mortar made from sharp sand and cement makes a wear-resistant mix for laying and pointing paving stones, but is too stiff and hard to be used for bricklaying.

Cement

The bonding agent that holds both concrete and mortar together. It is a caustic gray powder containing limestone, which crystallizes and hardens when mixed with water.

Ballast

A combination of gravel and sharp sand used in concrete mixes. A mix of 3:1 (three parts crushed stone or gravel and one part sharp sand) works well. It is also known as "aggregate."

Building sand

Sand with rounded grains used to make mortar. Because the grains are round, they roll over each other, making it easier to tap bricks and concrete blocks down to level. It also contains a small amount of clay, which makes it more pliable and sticky when wet.

Mortar and concrete mixes

Making concrete or mortar is like baking—you need a recipe and the ingredients in the right amounts. These are expressed as a ratio, for example 1:6, with the cement always first.

When mixing, always measure quantities using a leveled-off bucket, not a shovel. Because you are constantly making new mixes, consistency throughout the job ensures that concrete is strong and that the joints in the brickwork dry to the same color. To make concrete for a foundation, you need to make a 1:5 mix of cement and ballast. You can mix this by hand in a wheelbarrow or on a sheet of plywood, but it's easier and quicker with a cement mixer. To mix by hand, measure out five level buckets of ballast and place on a sheet of plywood. Sprinkle a bucket of cement over the top and turn with a shovel until the mix is an even gray color. Create a crater in the mix and lightly fill with water, turning in the edges until the mix is wet and soft, but not sloppy.

With a mechanical mixer, water is added first, followed by the cement, to form a slurry. This ensures that the ballast is completely coated as it is shoveled into the mixer. Add water with the ballast as necessary and mix for at least two minutes to obtain a uniform consistency.

Masonry mortar consists of 1:5 parts cement and building sand for work above ground and 1:3 for courses below ground. It can be mixed by hand as above, but for large jobs, rent a mechanical mixer to save

Mix mortar until the consistency is sticky.

time and effort. Add water until it becomes smooth but stiff enough to hold its shape when spread on a trowel. Once the right consistency has been achieved, work the mix for a few minutes to create small air bubbles in the mortar. These help to make it workable and sticky. A test to see whether it is the correct consistency for bricklaying is to scoop a little onto a trowel, shake off any excess, and turn the trowel upside down. If the mortar falls off, it needs more water or mixing.

Black mortar highlights the red bricks.

Additives are available, including dyes, which create colored joints in brickwork, and plasticizers, which increase the air bubble content of mortar, making mortar more forgiving to lay and easier to mix to the correct consistency. Plasticizers can be bought premixed into the cement or as liquid for adding as you mix.

Plasticizer increases the air bubble content of mortar.

Foundations

For walls under 3 ft. high, the depth of the concrete footing should be at least 8½ in. and never less than the thickness of the wall. The width of the foundation depends on how wide the wall is and whether or not it is a retaining wall. Freestanding walls require a footing between two and three times their width, while retaining walls demand a footing at least three times their width.

1 When digging the foundation, use lines to mark the width of the footing and dig down until you reach solid subsoil. The sides of the hole should be vertical, the ends square, and the base at least 4 in. deeper than the required depth of concrete (this allows the foundation to be buried out of sight).

2 Before pouring the concrete, hammer wood pegs along the center of the trench to the depth you want the concrete, and use a level to check that the pegs are all the same height. The pegs are a guide to help you make sure that the concrete is poured and smoothed to the correct level, making it strong and flat, which makes it much easier to lay bricks and blocks once it has dried.

3 Pour the concrete to the tops of the pegs, slicing with a shovel to release any trapped air. Screed to the tops of the pegs with a length of wood. Because the concrete shrinks as it hardens, let it set for forty-eight hours before starting construction.

slopes and DRAINAGE

Level changes, if enclosed by hedges or judiciously planted evergreens, can blur the boundaries of a garden, making it seem bigger, while at the same time hiding all but its best views and features. Boundaries across a slope can also create a sense of mystery. Where levels are changed, consideration has to be given to drainage.

Measuring slopes

One of the biggest worries for do-it-yourselfers is knowing the quantity of materials to order, or "quantifying." Provided that you have measured accurately, you will get all the help you need from your supplier. Measuring the length, height, and width of the boundary is easy, but it gets complicated if the ground slopes and you want to build a wall into it. To calculate the fall (how much the ground slopes), there are two methods.

Over a short distance, place a 6½-ft. straightedged plank at the top of the slope, and hold it out with a level on the top so it reaches over the bottom of the slope. When it's level with the base, then measure from the base to

Use a plank and a level to measure a fall.

the plank to give you the fall. For longer, gentler slopes, hammer in a post at the top of the slope, and then fix the top of the hose 3 ft. high on the post. Take the other end of the hose to the bottom of the slope and fill with water from a can. When it's full at both ends, they are level.

The fall is the measurement taken from the top of the hose to the ground at the bottom of the slope, less 3 ft. divided by its length.

Use a hose to measure a fall over long distances.

Fences and slopes

Picket, post-and-rail, and privacy fences can all be built to follow the contours of a slope perfectly. Panel fencing, because it comes in large 6-ft. sections, will not do this. Instead, it forms steps between each panel. Such

steps are useful for making particularly large jumps in level, however, they should be avoided, because they look unnatural and don't blend with the surroundings. If you have a slope, the choice is between a privacy or picket fence that undulates with the ground. If the slope is gentle, the fence can have a level top and an undulating base. Whichever you choose, always make the fence posts and the pickets or tapered boards upright, sloping only the rails, in order to produce a strong finished fence.

Walls and slopes

The large old walls surrounding grand houses were often built to follow the rises and falls in the land. Despite their longevity, such walls do not meet modern building standards, because they have shallow foundations and are stuck together with soft lime mortar. This seemingly weak construction actually accounts for their strength, allowing the wall to move as the soil shifts beneath their footings. The building of sloping walls is best left to specialists.

Retaining walls

While a gently rising lawn may be easy to live with, a patio needs to be level, and this means terracing into the slope and building retaining walls to hold back the soil.

Lining

If retaining walls aren't lined on the inside, the appearance of the bricks can be spoiled with a covering of white powder. This happens because water from the soil seeps into the bricks, carrying salt with it. When it reaches the face of the wall, the water evaporates and the salt is left behind. Water seeping through a wall will also make it vulnerable to algae, which looks particularly bad on plaster and will make it prone to being damaged by frost.

There are three ways to seal the back of a retaining wall from moisture. It can be given a coat of coal tar epoxy, which is a modern, quick-drying version of pitch. On the downside, it is expensive, and to get an even coat, the wall needs to be smooth.

Waterproof coal tar epoxy.

Another effective method of lining is to cover the back of the wall with a waterproof cement sand plaster available from any building supply store. It is time-consuming, but is a good way of sealing the wall and sloppy brickwork. Also, finishing on the back of the wall provides a good surface for

the plaster. The most economical way to seal the back of a wall is with a plastic vapor barrier. This tucks down against the wall and is held in place by the soil. Its only disadvantage is that it does not make a good seal around weep holes (see below).

Drainage

As well as holding back soil, a retaining wall slows down the movement of water. Unless adequate provision for drainage is included, the ground above the retaining wall will be wetter than it was before the wall was built.

Good drainage can be achieved in two ways. First, weep holes are lengths of $^3/_4$-in. plastic pipes cut to the width of the wall and laid every 3 ft. between bricks in the second course above ground level.

Lay weep holes between bricks in the second course.

A land drain is an attractive, if more complicated, option. This is a perforated, 4-in.-wide pipe set in gravel or sulfate-free hardcore on a slope of 1:70. The pipe connects to a land drain, known as a "soakaway," which consists of buried rubble that acts as a sump from which water is absorbed into the soil.

Lay the drainage pipe and connect with land drain.

Soakaways should be located near the end of the wall but always at least 16 ft. away from buildings and a good distance from utilities such as drains, sewers, and gas pipes. Whichever method you use, before backfilling the wall, line the soil behind it with landscape fabric. This is a fibrous material that keeps soil particles from blocking the drainage pipes.

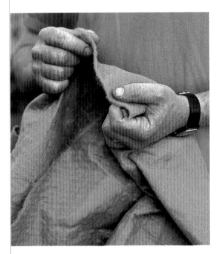

Landscape fabric.

Backfill the bottom half of the wall with a washed gravel or sulfate-free hardcore, and fold the landscape fabric over the top of it before filling to the top of the wall with soil.

bricks and BRICKLAYING

Bricklaying, like most crafts, involves many different skills that are simple on their own but, when put together, can seem daunting. However, by following the advice in this section and the projects on pages 42–57, you will be armed with all the knowledge you need to build freestanding and retaining garden walls up to 2 ft. high.

Brick types

Common bricks: Economical bricks with uneven color and texture manufactured for use where they won't be seen—for example, for use in foundation work, internal construction, and inside retaining walls.
Engineering bricks: Strong clay bricks with low water absorption for water-resistant courses and coping.
Facing bricks: Bricks with few blemishes and even color and surface texture manufactured for display.

Cutting bricks

Mark around the brick where you want to cut it and rest it on a layer of sand, edge-side up. Using a brick chisel and a hand sledge, strike the brick first on one edge then the other, going

Cutting bricks using a chisel and hand sledge.

back and forth between the two until it fractures in half.

Marking out

When building a brick wall, always chalk a line on the foundation to mark the face side and ends. To keep from having to cut bricks, make the length of the wall a multiple of the length of a brick, $8\frac{1}{2}$ in., plus the width of the joint, $\frac{1}{2}$ in. Calculate this on paper or lay a dry course of stretcher bricks (see box, next page) on the foundation, leaving $\frac{1}{2}$-in. spaces between them to get your dimensions.

Laying the first course

Next, set the end stretcher bricks in position on a trowel of mortar, tapping them down until the mortar beneath is $\frac{1}{2}$ in. thick and the tops are level with each other. Check this by bridging between them with a taut line or by resting a level on top of a straight-edged length of wood.

With the end bricks in place, run a line between them to mark their top front edge, holding it in position beneath two more bricks. This speeds up the rate of laying considerably, allowing the bricks in the center of the wall to be tapped level lengthwise by eye. You then only have to use a level to check across the wall.

Trowel mortar on the inside of the

line and ripple its surface by zigzagging the trowel's point along its length, creating a central channel. This spreads the mortar to the width of a brick and makes tapping the bricks level much easier.

Troweling mortar.

Buttering the end of a brick.

Turn the mortar to get plenty of air into it and trowel a small amount onto the end of the brick, smoothing the mortar to its edges. If the mortar keeps falling off, the mortar is too dry. Rectify this by splashing a small amount of water onto the mortar and turn it in with a trowel.

Laying subsequent courses

Position the buttered brick (see box at right) up to the line and push it against the end brick to create a $1/2$-in. joint between them. Tap each brick down until it is level front to back and its top edge is level with the line. Repeat this process until all of the face bricks are in place (the last brick will need to be buttered on both ends). Lay the bricks at the back of the wall, leaving a $1/2$-in. gap between the two skins (see box at right); check the level across the wall as you go. Fill the gap with mortar and start the next course with two header bricks, one at each end of the wall. Again, check that the joint is $1/2$-in.—a jointing tool (see page 33) is useful for this job—and run a line between the header bricks to mark their top edge. Cut a queen closure brick (see box at right) and lay this next to

Laying a queen closure brick.

break the vertical joint. Continue laying until the next course is complete.

Build up the ends of the wall first to support the builder's line and lay the bricks in the center, course by

Laying the second course.

course. As you work, collect the mortar that oozes out when the bricks are tapped down by running the point of the trowel along the face of the brick below, pulling excess mortar onto the trowel's blade. This, and any that falls onto the foundation, can be put back onto the mortar board for later use.

Leave any mortar that gets on the face of the bricks alone until it stiffens (this takes an hour or so, depending on the weather), then scrape it off with a trowel.

Pointing the joints

Next, "point" the joints, which involves smoothing over the dips and pits in the mortar to keep water out and to make the joints frostproof.

For walls in exposed positions, make what is called a "weather-struck joint" by pressing a pointing trowel held at an angle down the vertical joints, then across the vertical joints.

Weather-struck pointing.

using WOOD

Wood is a versatile, relatively inexpensive material, and you don't need the carpentry skills of a furniture maker to create beautiful wooden boundaries. With a few basic tools, a little know-how, and a can of colored wood stain, you can build a fence that captures the character of your garden while giving you and your plants shelter.

Wood joints

For many of the projects in this book, it is necessary to make simple joints to fasten lengths of wood together in a neat, strong way. While making joints takes a little time, it is easy to do and the finished result is far more attractive than when more expensive metal brackets are used.

Notch joints

These joints allow two pieces of wood to cross and yet still be flush with one another. They are useful when building gate frames and for notching the stringers of privacy fences into their supporting posts.

To make a notch joint

1 Lay the planks across one another and mark both pieces where you want the joint. Then mark the depth of the joint. This should be half the depth of the plank if they are the same size, or half the depth of the thinnest length.

2 To make chiseling the wood easier, make repeated cuts through each plank to the depth of the joint; leave approximately ½ in. between them. The fastest way to do this is with a circular saw set to the depth of the joint, but it is also easy to do with a wood saw.

3 Remove the remaining wood from the joint with a broad chisel.

Mortise joints

Basically, these joints involve one piece of wood slotting into another—like a key in a lock—and they are useful when making post-and-rail or privacy fences, where you want the posts to be visible from both sides, and for attaching picket fences to gate posts. To speed up the process, sharpen the ends of the stringers into points to reduce the amount of wood you need to chisel from the post.

1 Mark on the fence post where you want the joint to be positioned. Reduce its size if the stringers are sharpened as above.

2 Drill a series of holes through the post where you want the joint.

3 Chisel out the waste, slot in the stringers, and pin them in place with a nail or screw.

Fixing wood with screws and nails

To prevent wood from splitting, always drill pilot holes before tightening screws. To avoid constantly having to change the bits, borrow or rent an extra electric screwdriver so that you have one for the pilot bit and one for the screwdriver. Always use galvanized or coated nails and screws, because untreated types rust, leaving stains on the face of the wood.

Painting and preserving

Most store-bought fence panels are supplied pretreated with preservative for a life span of fifteen to twenty-five years. If you buy lumber to build your own custom fence, you can use untreated wood as long as you're prepared to coat it yourself with a wood stain or paint. That said, it always pays to buy pressure-treated wood for any part of the fence that will be in contact with the ground, such as posts and gravel boards. You can reduce the time it takes to paint a large fence by renting a paint sprayer. It's ideal for painting trellises, as well.

Fences and trees

If there is a tree growing along the line where you want to build a fence, don't nail the fence directly to it, because when the tree sways in the wind, so will the fence. If this happens, the fence and the tree could both be damaged. Instead, put a post a yard or so back from the trunk and cantilever two stringers to within several inches of it. For effect, a false post can go on the end, propped in place by a diagonal plank spiked into the ground behind the tree. Where there are branches, dips or holes can be cut in the fence, allowing room for the tree

Situate posts well back from trees.

to move in the wind. In this way, instead of an inconvenience, the tree will give your fence character.

Cutting down a fence panel

At the end of a fence run, it is often necessary to cut down a panel in order to turn a corner or connect the fence with a building.

1 Draw a line down the fence where you want the cut.
2 Screw a length of $\frac{3}{4} \times 2$ in. batten to each side of the fence along the line.
3 Cut the fence down with a saw.

Sawing the fence panel to size.

Curved fences

To create a curve, use wood thin enough to be bent into an arc for the stringers. To give the stringers strength and to hold their shape, they need to be laminated. Bend them around a series of posts temporarily hammered into the ground around the arc and attach the stringers to the two end posts with screws. Paint the outer face with external wood glue and bend another length of wood over the top. Screw it in place as you go. Allow the glue to set, then detach and fix into position.

Fence jargon

Gravel boards—Commonly used to underpin panel and privacy fences. They form a barrier between the ground and the main fence, taking all the weather and rotting first.

Stringers—Sometimes called "arris rails," these are planks that run between the posts and have pickets or tapered boards hammered to them.

Tapered boards—Wood planks that are wedge-shaped in cross section to allow them to overlap each other.

incorporating PLANTS

Plants bring seasonality, character, and individuality to even the most mundane spaces, and they deserve as much thought and care as any boundary detail. This section will help you choose the right plants for your boundaries so that they get off to the best possible start.

Hedges

Planting a hedge is the quickest and most economical way to enclose a large area. Before planting, dig along the line of your intended hedge, incorporating a wheelbarrow load of garden compost, well-rotted horse manure, or store-bought soil improver every 13–16 ft. Then, plant your hedge, firm the roots, and water well.

The trick to getting hedges to establish quickly is to water through the growing season, particularly during dry spells in the first year after planting. To encourage the hedge to fill out, lightly trim the sides in early summer of the second year. Although it's tempting to plant the hedge and simply leave it to grow to the height

A smart, low front garden hedge.

you want before cutting it back, it's better to trim its top half a few feet below the desired height. This will encourage it to branch out and fill out more quickly. Once the hedge is at the desired height, it will be easier to trim, because cutting back prevents the formation of thick, tough branches.

With most hedges, you can get away with one major pruning at the end of summer. This gives them time to put on a fresh set of leaves for winter, while removing unwanted growth. For the neatest look, especially with hedges such as boxwood (*Buxus*), yew (*Taxus*), and topiary features, it's best to give a quick prune after the last frost in late spring and then again in late summer. When trimming hedges over 3–4 ft., always make the sides slope inward slightly to give the hedge an A-shaped profile. Otherwise, the top of the hedge will cast a shadow over the base, making it gappy.

Climbers and wall shrubs

To soften brand-new fences and walls, climbers and wall shrubs are the obvious choice. The range is vast, so first decide what features you want your climber to have—flowers, berries, scent, evergreen, or deciduous, perhaps some fall color? Most of us want all of these things, but that's

Climbers soften the square edges of a panel fence.

impossible from just one plant. However, by combining a couple of plants, you can have it all. Next decide what will grow in front of the boundary. Even if you are unsure of your gardening knowledge, garden centers and nurseries can help you choose if you know the following:
• Aspect—Which way does the site face? Does it catch morning or afternoon sun, or none at all?
• Soil—Sandy and free-draining, or clay and sticky? Take a sample to the garden center for advice.
• Exposure—Is it very hot and prone to dry out? Is wind a factor?
• What do the neighbors grow well, because often similar plants will do well for you.

• Size and space—How much area do you need to fill, including base and top?
• How wet or dry is the soil? Does it collect puddles in winter and crack in the heat of summer, or is it always boggy or dry?

Keep in mind that climbers grow in different ways. Clematis (*Clematis*) establishes on top of a support, forming a cloud of foliage and flowers, so fill the gap with herbaceous perennials or smaller shrubs such as lavender (*Lavandula*). Honeysuckle (*Lonicera*) and jasmine (*Jasminum*) become great, sprawling mounds in front of a support. They often look their best when they cascade over from the other side, so they are a good choice for internal divides. Wisteria (*Wisteria*), climbing roses (*Rosa*), and grape vines (*Vitis*) all lend themselves to training, allowing you to cover the boundary as you want.

If you are building around a well-established plant, then you can always plan for it in your boundary design.

A scalloped wall to highlight the position of a tree.

Planting at the base of a boundary

Life at the base of a wall or fence is harsh—it is potentially sheltered from rain and what moisture there is can be sapped up by the boundary. Give plants a good start by digging in lots of garden compost or store-bought soil improver to increase the soil's water-holding capacity. This will also help drainage in wetter soils. Plants bought in containers won't grow into the surrounding soil for a few weeks, so they need a reservoir of easily accessible water.

Before planting, soak the rootball in a bucket of water until the air has bubbled out. Dig your hole at least 20 in. from the base of the boundary to enable the plant to root into better soil and to give the roots space to grow. Sometimes it's hard to give plants enough water, so cut a plastic bottle in half, take off its lid, and sink it into the soil. It will act like a funnel, directing water to the roots.

This plastic bottle directs water down to the roots.

Supports or self-clinging

Some climbers, like Virginia creeper (*Parthenocissus quinquefolia*), climbing hydrangea (*Hydrangea anomala petiolaris*), and ivy (*Hedera*) are self-clinging and need only to be directed toward the boundary to pull themselves up. Others, like roses, passionflower (*Passiflora*), and honeysuckle, require a support to wind around. Wires fixed at 18-in. intervals horizontally up the support are a far better choice than trellises. Unless it's used carefully, a trellis can spoil the look of a boundary and is unsuitable for many climbers. Wires, on the other hand, are discreet and versatile. They run in any direction and are easier to remove if necessary. Some climbers, such as clematis and honeysuckle, will weave in front of and behind the wire, but when you are training climbers, try to avoid tucking stems behind the wires, because it makes them difficult to move later.

Fixing vine eyes

Wires need to be held on a support with 4–6 in. hooks called "vine eyes" that are screwed into the boundary. These hold the climber about 2 in. away from the support and allow air to circulate behind, helping to prevent mildew and other fungal diseases. Always choose plastic-coated wires, and tighten them in place using bolt tensioners at the end of each horizontal wire. Or, you can use vine eyes on their own to pin individual stems in place by tying the branches to each vine eye with soft twine.

good WORKING PRACTICE

When all of your time is spent moving things out of the way or looking for tools, construction jobs become disorganized, and the fun of building is lost. Organizing your tools and materials before starting a project is essential and enables you to carry out the job swiftly, safely, and with good results, so that you can enjoy yourself.

Personal safety

Your own safety and the safety of others is the primary consideration when building any garden project. To protect yourself, wear strong gloves when handling materials with sharp or splintered edges, such as stone, brick, and wood, and always wear them when handling cement. Safety goggles are essential when cutting stone and bricks, and should be combined with a mask when spray painting. One of the most common injuries occurs when tools or heavy materials fall on your feet, so always wear steel-toed boots. To protect your back, lift properly: face the object and pick it up with your knees bent and your back straight. Finally, don't overdo it. If you're not accustomed to physical work, take your time, and if possible, find others to help you. As with most gardening jobs, working with someone else always more than doubles the speed at which the job is done, especially when doing hard manual work such as digging foundations or carrying materials.

Site safety

Because boundaries tend to be relatively large, you're going to have to bring a lot of materials into your garden. Ensure easy access by tying back shrubs and trees that could get in your way when materials are wheelbarrowed through, and use planks of wood supported on bricks to ramp up low steps. Taking your time to make the access to your

Use planks as ramps on steps.

garden as open as possible will make carrying the materials easier and safer.

Treat moving materials as a separate job from the construction. Stack materials in stable piles close to where you will be needing them. Doing this prevents unnecessary legwork during construction and means the materials won't topple over.

If you or your neighbors have children and you are replacing a perimeter boundary, the children must be considered at all times. To a child, a stack of bricks, power tools, chisels, and hammers presents an irresistible opportunity for fun. Make sure that tools are kept well out of their reach. If necessary, cordon off your working area with a temporary plastic fence.

Always lift with your knees bent.

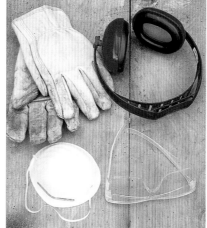
Safety equipment.

Safety and protection

Always lift properly with your knees bent and your back straight.

Be sure to wear steel-toed boots.

When cutting stone and bricks, always wear goggles.

Wear strong gloves when handling materials with sharp or splintered edges.

Keep all tools well out of the reach of children and cordon off your working area with a temporary plastic fence.

Tools

The list of tools you need is included with each of the projects. If you don't own them, rent them—the extra cost is worth paying, because it will make building much easier. If you rent tools, book them a few days before you need them, along with any necessary attachments like saw blades and safety equipment. When they are delivered, read the instructions and spend a little time practicing how to use them.

Be sure that all the tools you need are in working order. At the end of each day, clean the tools and store

Cleaning off a trowel at the end of the day.

them away in a secure place where you can get to them easily.

Organizing your work

Give yourself plenty of room so you can work comfortably. Do this by assigning different jobs involved in the construction of your boundary to different parts of your garden. For example, create a space for a workbench that allows you to move freely around it, especially if you are cutting wood. Allocate another for mixing mortar. This should be near where the sand is delivered, in an open spot that is easy to carry materials to and from using a wheelbarrow, and where splashes of cement from the mixer won't cause any damage. For projects such as building trellises, screens, and gates, you also need a space to lay them flat while you work. This can be a patio, driveway, or lawn, but it should be as close as possible to the final location.

As you work, stand back from the job regularly to check that string lines are level and in the correct place, and to help you plan the next stage. The trick to building things well is to be methodical and to give yourself plenty of time to enjoy what is a creative process. Give yourself time to make sure each stage is finished properly before beginning the next.

Another thing to remember before cutting anything to length, whether it is wood, metal, or stone, is the old adage "measure twice and cut once."

Leaving the job

At the end of the day, clean off tools—in particular, those that have been used for concreting or bricklaying, before the cement dries and hardens. Open bags should be

Place open bags of cement in trash bags.

placed into trash bags and brought into a shed or garage for the night. Protect concrete footings, walls, and unopened bags of cement from rain with plastic sheets. It's also good practice to cover stacked bricks and blocks, because mortar sticks to them more readily when they are dry. Cordon off any excavations with brightly colored marker tape, or cover them with wood boards. Lock away tools and equipment.

Cordon off foundations with marker tape.

tools and
EQUIPMENT

With the right tools, you're halfway there to getting the job done quickly and well. Some tools, such as spades, are a good investment, because they are sure to be used time and again, while others can be rented for specific jobs. The tools have been split into categories: groundwork, masonry and bricklaying, carpentry, and those suitable for renting.

Groundwork tools

Sledgehammer This long-handled and weighty hammer is a crude but very effective tool. Its uses range from simple demolition to driving fence spikes into the ground to tamping concrete around the base of posts.

Ground-marking paint A water-based aerosol paint for marking out plans and fence lines on the ground. A good aid for visualizing designs before starting work.

Bamboo stakes Useful for setting out the features in a garden plan before construction starts.

Mattock This tool looks like a pickax and can be used for digging, but it also has a flat blade that is perfect for scooping soil from trenches and a blade that is useful for chopping through old roots.

Measuring tape This is useful for garden surveying and speeding up the marking of a design on the ground.

Fencing bar An iron bar used for making holes in the ground and breaking through buried stones.

Wheelbarrow An essential piece of equipment used for all construction. Choose a model with a pneumatic tire and a metal bucket. Buy from a building supply store, as wheelbarrows stocked by garden centers are often too weak for construction work.

Masonry and bricklaying tools

Brick chisel A steel tool with a wide, blunt blade for cutting bricks, concrete blocks, and stone.

Hand sledge A heavy hammer for demolition and for driving a chisel when cutting bricks.

Builder's line A strong woven line for marking out levels when laying bricks or for the tops of fence posts. It can be tensioned to make straight lines.

Level A tool for all fence and wall construction that enables them to be built perfectly upright. There are long ones for finding horizontal lines over a wide area, short ones for working in confined spaces, and 90° levels with two sets of bubbles used for positioning over the corner of a fence post to indicate if it leans to the left or to the right or front to back.

Builder's pins These are pointed metal pegs that can be driven between bricks or into the ground for tying off a builder's line.

Pointing trowel This is a small, triangular-shaped trowel used for smoothing the joints of brickwork.

Bucket Essential for accurately measuring quantities of sand and cement by volume, pouring water, and rinsing off dirty tools at the end of each day.

Mortar board A mortar board for block- or bricklaying is usually made from a square piece of plywood approximately 2 x 2 ft. It acts as a place to pile mortar within reaching distance of where you are working, and forms a convenient flat surface from which to load the trowel.

Jointing tool A gauge made from a scrap of wood that is used to check that mortar joints in a wall are the correct depth. It is particularly useful when it comes to building walls with two skins, because it helps to keep their joints at the same height as they are built.

Carpentry tools

Beetle A crude-looking rustic mallet, traditionally carved from the branch of an elm tree. Custom tools such as these are no longer commonplace, but they are a delight to use because they can be weighted perfectly for their purpose and the person using them.

Wood chisel Available in various sizes and used for cutting and squaring wood joints. For fencing joints, a ³/₄-in. blade is fine. Keep the blade sharp and work with a wooden mallet—metal ones are hard to use accurately and will crack the handle.

Circular saw The ideal tool for cross-cutting wood to length and for cutting planks into strips. It comes with a metal guide bar (fence), which clips over the edge of the plank, keeping the blade straight. This saw is battery-powered, so you can use it away from a source of electricity, but it is less powerful. If you are cutting thick wood and have access to electricity, rent an electric model.

Jigsaw A useful electric saw for cutting curved and straight lines. It comes with interchangeable blades for sawing wood, plastic, and sheet metal. The trick to accurate cutting with a jigsaw is to look over its top at the blade while working. Doing this allows you to guide the saw more easily and adjust its position if it strays from the line.

Mallet A wooden hammering tool for driving wood chisels and for knocking wood joints and fence posts into position without scarring them.

Hand saw An all-purpose saw for cutting wood to length.

Workbench Choose a model with a large top and clamps for holding materials while you work.

Ground Fault Circuit Interrupter Sometimes known as a "circuit breaker," an GFCI is an essential piece of safety equipment for use with all electrical power tools. It can switch off the supply of electricity if it detects that the power cable has been cut or the tool has developed a fault, thus reducing the risk of electrocution. The power tool is simply plugged into the GFCI, which in turn is plugged into an electrical socket.

Router A power tool with a spinning blade, used for beveling the edges of wooden boards. Different blades can be used to achieve a range of finishes.

Surform A tool used for planing wood. It has a blade reminiscent of a cheese grater—ideal for removing sharp edges from wooden boards.
T square This is a square that is used for woodworking.

Rental equipment

Any tool can be rented hourly or daily, from screwdrivers all the way up to tractor-mounted excavators. To save money, only rent tools as you need them, and choose a rental agency that will deliver and collect the tools when you are finished with them. When renting equipment with a gas engine, such as a cement mixer or auger, check whether fuel is supplied; if you don't own one already, rent a fuel can to keep it topped up.

All mechanical rental equipment comes with safety instructions, and it is your responsibility to read them. Safety equipment, such as protective goggles, ear protectors, and dust masks, is often supplied separately.

Although renting tools will make any job more expensive, they will save time and will reduce tedious or arduous work such as digging holes for fence posts or foundations.
Cement mixer Mixing concrete and cement by hand is a backbreaking job that a mechanical mixer will do for you. Always rent an electric mixer if you will have access to a power supply, because they are quieter than gas models and easier to start.

Fencing spoons An ingenious, long-handled excavating tool for digging deep, steep-sided holes for fence posts, these are inexpensive to rent and a real time-saver.

Paint sprayer An inexpensive tool to rent that will save hours of brushwork (days even, if you're painting trellises) and reduce the amount of paint you use. Always wear a mask.

Power auger The fastest way to dig a line of holes for fence posts is with a power auger. As the blade turns, it screws into the ground, pushing out the soil. You have to be strong to use one alone, but most can be operated by two people.

Trenching spade A reinforced spade with a flat blade for digging straight-sided holes and foundations. Rent if your plans require a lot of digging.

Turf remover Worth renting if you are creating borders next to a boundary or making over a whole garden. It will save you the blisters and time it takes to cut away grass by hand.

Equipment

Decorative nails Thick iron nails with ornamental heads that give a studded finish to gates. They can be bought in various lengths and rustproofed to prevent black stains from developing as the iron reacts to the wood. Because they have wide shanks, they need pilot holes to keep the wood from splitting. To clamp lengths of wood together, use long nails and bend the ends over.

Drainage pipe (4 in.) This collects water through holes in its side. It is laid underground in a bed of gravel or sulfate-free hardcore—sulfate salts would clog it up—and connects to a land drain. To carry water effectively, drainage pipes must be laid with a slope of ½ in. for every 35 in. in length.

Fencing spikes These are metal sockets for fixing fence posts. As well as spikes for hammering into soil, they can have plates or wings for bolting/setting in concrete, and short wedge-shaped spikes, which are hammered down the sides of broken fence posts to repair them.

Hinges and latches There are many different types available, and your choice will depend on whether you want them to be discreet or decorative. For outdoor use, though, always go for those protected with rustproof paint.

Fence spike driving tool A protective plastic block that is inserted into the socket of the fence spike while it is driven into the ground.

Staples C-shaped nails used for fixing wires and screen cladding to fences. Always choose galvanized staples, because they won't rust.

Brick ties Loops or lengths of curved, galvanized wire that are laid between courses and used to lock walls made of two independent skins of brick- or block work together.

Using these tool lists

To prevent repetitive lists of tools from appearing at the end of each project, only the necessary tool categories (masonry and bricklaying, for example) have been recorded. If any item from another section is also required to complete the project, it is listed individually. Any necessary rental equipment is also shown.

walls

planning walls

When you visit the gardens of a stately old home, many of the garden rooms are inevitably enclosed by venerable old walls—the details of the mortar and the patterns of the brick are like laugh lines on a character-filled face. Long-lasting and solid, walls impart a feeling of permanence and reassurance, regardless of whether the place is new or ancient.

Function and style This book concentrates on low walls, because they are most manageable for do-it-yourself work and don't stray into the area that requires planning permission. Consequently, these walls are most suited to either front yards or low internal boundaries around patios and sunken gardens. Many also make good retaining walls, suitable for creating terraces and level areas on sloping sites. They can also double up as seating.

The materials used for walls are many, from traditional bricks, stone, and wood to more modern reclaimed railroad ties and gabions. The material you use depends on your budget, ability, and the style that suits you and your space. The larger the basic element of the wall, the quicker it is and the less skill it takes to build. However, you must keep in mind that building with large units, like railroad ties, is often a two-person job. You may want to spend more time later on detailing, such as coping or planting. The other advantage is that larger units are cheaper.

On the other hand, small units are far more versatile for creating curved and serpentine boundaries. They look good as internal screens, because they disguise the perimeter and lead your eye into the center of the garden.

Design choices Walls are either formal or informal in appearance, depending on the material used in their construction and finish. At one end of the scale, a smooth plastered wall coated with a glossy paint has a crisp, man-made look. At the other extreme, a randomly stacked stone wall with plants cascading from between the rocks presents a much softer, natural face. In between, mixing old and new, are adaptable materials such as gabions.

Stone, when laid in definite courses, can look architectural enough to blend with buildings, while at the same time soft

Stone wall of various heights.

Old-style garden wall.

A wall to harmonize with the house.

Dry stone wall planter.

One of the most common uses for walls is to hold back soil (top left). Such walls make excellent seats and shelves for container plants. Low walls also create interesting internal divides, separating a path from a gravel garden or retaining the soil adjacent to a stepped path (top right and above).

Country meets classical—the undulating face of this dry-stacked stone wall contrasts beautifully with the straightedged pier.

enough to harmonize with the plantings of the garden as a whole. A soil-filled dry stone wall is more like a hedge than a wall, because of the way it becomes festooned with plants.

Plastered and brick walls both blend effortlessly with houses. Depending on the finish and color of the brick or plaster, they can create a cottage garden, city, or even Mediterranean theme. Plus, there are plenty of homespun details that can give a wall personal character, such as incorporating bottle ends during construction.

A low wall is the strongest of any physical enclosure, even if it is no more than 3 ft. high. This is especially the case around a patio. Because you are normally sitting down, anything solid that's higher could make the space feel oppressive. However, that should not prevent you from placing lighter screens on top of the wall (picket fencing or clouds of plants, for example).

Types of wall
Brick—There are thousands of different types of brick and various patterns in which to lay them. Warm and established in character, brick works well near houses or outbuildings. There are also special bricks for coping and corners.

Plastered—Plaster can give an ugly wall a new lease on life, or give an economically made concrete block wall an expensive, up-to-the-minute finish. It's a chameleon, fitting neatly with cottage gardens, city spaces, and sun-baked Moroccan-style courtyards. Leave rough for a mud wall look, smooth for a crisp urban finish, or undulate the surface to replicate the appearance of the plastered stone walls of a Moroccan villa.

Railroad ties—Railroad ties are becoming more and more popular, not just for walls, but also for steps and paths. They are straightforward to lay and their warm, chunky look accommodates all styles of gardens.

Stone—Sandstone and limestone are the most common types of stone used for walls. They can be bought as random or "dressed" boulders (shaped into blocks). Dressed stone creates a wall with regimented courses and is easier to lay, while random stone has a more rustic appearance, unless it is carefully placed and put together like a jigsaw puzzle for an Asian feel.

Gabions—Gabions have long been used to shore up banks and the sides of waterways. However, since metal has become more popular in a garden setting, gabions have been given a new spin with more interesting types and colors of stone, such as slate.

This plastered concrete block wall (above left), painted in warm terra cotta, is the perfect backdrop to the cypress and citrus trees in this Mediterranean-themed garden. The concrete block raised pond (above right) is softened with plaster and painted vibrant red. It has an almost plastic look and makes a lively contrast to the soft plants at its base and the curly-leaved sedge in the water.

Rammed earth wall.

Contoured paving stone.

Gabion wall.

Chunky stacked wood.

railroad tie WALL

Railroad ties have a myriad of uses in the garden, and they make attractive low walls that are quick to build. Their wood is warm and chunky, and when used for a retaining wall, it doubles up as a seat and a place to display pots of flowers.

1 | Mark out the position of the railroad tie wall and excavate roughly 12 in. of soil from the bank to give you room to work behind the wall. Level and firm the ground before laying the bottom course of ties on edge. The railroad ties then act like a guide, helping you to locate the positions of the 2 x 2 in. wood pegs that support them. Hammer one peg into the soil every 3 ft., driving it in until it is about 3 in. lower than the finished height of the wall. When cutting pegs to length, make sure that the points on their ends are even, otherwise, they will tilt when driven into the ground.

2 | Where the railroad ties meet at a corner, mark and cut them with a saw so that they fit together perfectly. To be sure that your cuts are straight, mark right around the railroad tie to guide you as you saw through the wood. As you stack the ties back in position, make sure that the

1 Having laid the first course of railroad ties on edge and backfilled with soil, hammer pegs behind them as a support.

2 Next mark and cut the railroad ties that meet at a corner. Doing this gives a much neater, flush finish.

KNOW YOUR MATERIALS

Because reclaimed railroad ties are impregnated with tar, they are unsuitable for use as a seat or anywhere you might brush up against them and get tar on your clothes. For this reason, it is much better to buy new railroad ties that are made from untreated larch or pine, because they are clean and can either be painted to match the color scheme in your garden or left to become sun-bleached white, as seen in this project. If you do choose to use reclaimed railroad ties, always buy grade 1 ties—they are graded 1–3, according to their condition—and avoid any with gummy patches of tar. Also, cover their tops with strips of wood.

joints between the second course of ties don't overlap with the first, so that the two courses lock together.

3 With the ties back in their final position, use a level to check that they are upright and fix them in place with 4-in screws driven through the back of each peg into the ties. Backfill with soil and plant behind the wall. Then lay decking or gravel at its base.

Drainage

Joints in railroad tie walls aren't sealed, and allow excess water in the soil behind them to escape. Therefore, they don't need drainage holes or pipes to take the water away.

Tall retaining walls

For walls above knee height, increase width and strength by laying the railroad ties on their sides. Walls taller than 3 ft. should have a 15° lean into the soil behind. Drill holes through ties and link with mild steel rods.

3 Once the railroad ties are in position, drive a screw through the back of each peg into the ties. Finally, backfill with soil and plants.

stone planter WALL

A stone wall is the ultimate custom boundary, because every single rock is unique and no two people would lay them in the same way. In addition to the warmth and inherent charm of the stone, practically speaking you cannot get a more solid boundary than this.

1 | This wall differs from other rustic stone walls you may have seen, because soil is packed into its center. This means that plants can root into it, creating a colorful garden feature as well as a boundary.

Mark out the base of the wall on the ground using sand or ground-marking paint. Make the width 24 in., and for strength give it a curved or serpentine shape. Then use a spade to dig out the top 6 in. of soil to give you a firm, even base to build from. Pile the soil close by for use later on.

2 | Before building, organize your work area by laying out as many stones as space allows so that you can quickly pick and choose between them. It is important to note that once a stone is picked up, it should never be put down unless it's in the wall. Although you won't get it right every time, even after practice, it does make a lot of

MATERIALS

Dressed stone blocks

Topsoil

Plants

Irrigation hose

TOOLS

Masonry and bricklaying tools

Spade

Length of wood

Brick hammer

1 After deciding upon the shape and size of your wall, mark out the base on the ground and dig out 6 in. of soil.

2 Lay the first course of stones along both edges of the footing, fitting them together snugly.

KNOW YOUR MATERIALS

There is an old saying—"stone for walls doesn't travel far"—that is as true today as it ever was because hauling costs are so high. So when it comes to choosing stone, always source it locally to save money and to ensure that it blends with your surroundings. This is less of an issue if you live in a city, where its use in residential buildings is limited. However, if you already have stone in your garden, try to match the wall with it; otherwise, there is a risk that your garden will become a hodgepodge of different materials that lack harmony. Always ask your supplier to help quantify how much stone you'll need, because the amount will vary according to the size and type of stone used.

sense to do as much sorting and choosing by eye as possible. Start the wall by placing stones of similar height along both edges of the wall, leaving space between them—the two layers of stone plus the space between them should measure 24 in.

3 Fill the space between the stones with the soil from the base, packing it down firmly with a length of wood. I like for grass to grow from the sides of soil-filled stone walls, because it softens the edges of the stone. However, if you prefer a crisper appearance, weed out any grass roots or use weed-free topsoil instead.

4 Lay the second row of stones, staggering the joints with the first, and gently slope the face of each stone toward the center of the wall. If each course is laid in this way, the wall will be A-shaped in profile, which increases its strength because the two faces prop each other up. When laying this course, deliberately leave planting gaps every few stones. Putting the plants in at this level gives

them room to trail. To further strengthen the wall, bridge long stones every yard or so between the two faces to tie them together. Then pack with soil as before.

5 As you build, try to make the ends of the stones fit snugly together (except where you want planting holes). Any sharp points or lumps can be chipped away with a brick hammer or chisel.

6 If any of the stones rock or if any of the gaps are large, use slithers of stone to wedge them in place or to bridge spaces. If you don't have enough small pieces, go to Step 8 and cut a few coping stones to create some.

Another method of locking the stones together is to use mortar between the gaps on the inside of the wall where it won't be seen. It is particularly useful for fixing stones with difficult rounded edges and for giving stonework adjacent to entrances rigidity. Use a 1:4 cement and sharp sand mix and work into the gaps between the stones with a pointing trowel (see page 33).

3 Ram soil between the stones using a length of wood. This packs the stones in position and creates a firm base.

4 When laying the second course, place long stones between the two faces to strengthen the wall.

5 To fit the stones together snugly, chip off sharp points or lumps from the ends using a brick hammer or chisel.

7 | Before planting, stand the pots in a bucket of water to ensure that the rootball is wet. Remove the plants from their containers and wedge them between the stones, firming soil from the heart of the wall around them. In this wall, houseleeks (*Sempervivum carneum*), sedums (*Sedum*), sea pinks (*Armeria maritima*), and saxifrages (*Saxifraga*) were planted in sweeps and drifts, as though they had colonized the gaps between the stones over time, to give the wall an old-world appearance. For a lush effect, you could use low-growing grasses such as gray-leaved fescues (*Festuca*) and yellow sedges (*Carex*), or a traditional alpine mix including blue aubrieta (*Aubrieta*) and yellow alyssum (*Lobularia*). Alternately, plant grass seed between the stones for a natural country look.

8 | Continue to build up the wall, leaving gaps and planting as you go along, tying the two faces together with long stones as before and packing the wall with soil. For the final course, don't use any long stones and simply pack

with soil. This allows enough space for an irrigation hose to be placed in the top (see pages 108–9 for details).

To make a coping, cut the stone into 1–2 in. slices by laying it on the ground and striking with a hand sledge and brick chisel along the strata. It is easy to do if you cut the stones in half and half again until they are the width you want. If you try to take off the slices from one side of the stone only, the tensions inside it will cause it to fracture.

Alternative ideas

For stability, a stone planter wall shouldn't be over 4 ft. high, but if you want to build one as a perimeter boundary for privacy, you can adjust the design so that a hedge can be grown in the top. Do this by making the wall shorter and wider, about 2 × 3 ft. Good plants for this are native hedge row trees such as hawthorn (*Crataegus*) and elderberry (*Sambucus*), with woodbine (*Lonicera periclymenum* 'Belgica' and 'Serotina') scrambling through it.

6 *Use slithers of stone to fill any gaps and to wedge any stones that move or rock firmly into the wall.*

7 *When laying the second course, leave planting gaps between the stones. Firm plant roots into the soil in the center of the wall.*

8 *Having laid the final course, split the stone to make a coping, using a hand sledge and brick chisel.*

plastered block WALL

The vivid paint colors in modern garden designs, such as Mediterranean blue and earthy ocher, have given plastered walls a new lease on life. They are once again held in high regard for their smart, flawless finish, and yet they are surprisingly easy to build.

1 | Use ground-marking paint to mark out the position of the wall on the soil, and lay the foundation (see page 21 for details on specifications). Screed the surface of the concrete foundation slab flat with a length of wood and allow it to dry for at least forty-eight hours before building so that the concrete has fully hardened.

2 | Organize your building area by stacking blocks within easy reach of the face of the wall, and set a wood mortar board on a few blocks next to where you're starting. If you are building a curved wall (like the one pictured opposite), cut some of the blocks in half. To do this, rest a block on soft ground and strike it with a hand sledge and brick chisel right around where you want to make the cut. Making the blocks smaller in this way allows you to create a smoother arc on the curve.

MATERIALS

High-density concrete blocks

Ballast

Cement

Soft sand

½-in. plastic pipe for weep holes

Coal tar epoxy

Plastic vapor barrier

TOOLS

Groundwork tools

Masonry and bricklaying tools

Metal and plastic float

Wood mortar board

1 Once you have marked the position of the wall on the ground, lay the foundation. Use wood to screed the surface of the concrete flat.

2 Use a hand sledge and brick chisel to cut some blocks in half—smaller blocks allow you to create a smoother arc on the curve.

KNOW YOUR MATERIALS

Plaster is tremendously versatile and can be used to achieve dozens of effects. Smoothed and painted, it can have all the shine of plastic. If left rough, with the lines of the float still showing, it has the appearance of compacted soil. For a weathered stone effect, smooth the plaster into gentle undulations and coat with earthy-colored paint. The coping also affects the look. Bricks and polished paving stones are crisp and clean, while wood decking creates a seaside feel. For a jungle look, round the plaster over the top of the wall, creating the illusion that the wall is made from mud. Give it a coat of spicy ginger-colored paint and plant large-leaved palms and grasses behind.

3 Laying concrete blocks is easier than laying bricks, but the principles are exactly the same. Work from the face side of the wall, building the ends of the straight sections first and running taut lines between them to give you the level of each course (see page 24 for details). Then build up the curves using a level and matching them with the straight sections. Start by mixing a 1:5 cement and soft sand mortar and lay the blocks onto this, tapping down until the joints are ½ in. deep and the blocks are level. Buttering the end of each block with mortar (see page 25 for details) and pushing it up against the last block is the correct way to lay them, but if you struggle while doing this, use a pointing trowel to fill the gaps with mortar afterward.

4 On the second course, angle plastic weep holes downward from the back of the wall. These drainage pipes should be set into the mortar between the blocks every 3 ft. Cut the pipes so that the ends protrude at least ¾ in. beyond the face of the wall to make space for the plaster. Alternately, lay a drainage pipe along the back of the wall (see page 23 for details).

5 As long as the joints of each course are staggered, your pointing doesn't matter. In fact, the rougher it is, the better surface it gives the plaster. For strength, though, the wall must be level both across the tops of the blocks and up the face of the wall. Check this by placing a level up against its face as you build.

6 When the wall is complete, let it set for forty-eight hours. Then mix up a plaster consisting of 1:8 parts cement and soft sand (make this slightly stiffer than the mortar used in the blockwork). Place a flat board at the foot of the wall to catch any dropped plaster. Working up from the base, smear the plaster onto the wall using a metal float. Aim to keep the depth of the plaster roughly ½ in. To create an edge to work to at the top of the wall, hold a length of wood or another float so that it overhangs the face of the wall by ½ in. This allows you to

3 When the straight sections have been laid, butter mortar on the ends of the half blocks for the curves and lay them in place.

4 On the second course, make weep holes by setting drainage pipes into the mortar between the blocks at 3-ft. intervals.

5 As you go along, keep checking that the wall is level across the tops of the blocks and up the face of the wall.

scrape the plaster off the float and ensures that its top is flush with the top of the wall.

7　When the wall is complete, allow it to dry for twenty minutes or so before smoothing over the surface with a plastic float. For a really flat finish, work the float in a circular motion until all of the dips and lines are filled. Then, smooth around the drainage weep holes with a pointing trowel. Alternately, for an earthy Mediterranean effect, just take off the worst peaks.

8　Allow the plaster to dry for twenty-four hours before laying the coping stones on top of the wall. These sit on a bed of 1:5 cement and soft sand mortar. Lay them in a similar way to the blocks, tap them so that they are level, and use a trowel to catch any mortar that oozes over the face of the wall. Then fill the gaps between them with mortar. Paint the wall and lay gravel to hide the drainage holes. At the back of the wall, paint coal tar epoxy around the weep holes and line it with a plastic

vapor barrier (see page 22), cutting slits for each hole. Backfill with washed gravel to a depth of 12 in., separating it from the soil with landscape fabric—this stops fine particles from blocking up the drainage holes. Then backfill with soil to the top of the wall and plant.

Applying plaster

If you are building a plastered wall next to a border, make sure that the base of the plaster sits an inch above soil level. This prevents the plaster from soaking up groundwater, which leads to algae forming on the face of the wall and increases the risk of frost damage. On curved sections of a wall, mark a neat line along the base of the plaster with a pointing trowel and scrape it away before it dries. On straight walls, attach a length of 1/2-in. wood batten with screws just above soil level height, then apply the plaster using the wood as a base. Once the plaster is dry, the wood can be removed.

6 To ensure that the top of the plaster is flush with the top of the wall, hold a float so that it overhangs the face of the wall.

7 After the wall is complete, smooth over the surface with a plastic float and use a pointing trowel to smooth around the weep holes.

8 When the plaster is dry, lay the coping stones on top of the wall, tapping them down so they are level.

gabion WALL

Traditionally used in sea defenses, these stone-filled steel cages suit modern garden designs very well, striking the required balance between the natural and the man-made. They are also easy to build and an economical way to create a sturdy, low wall.

1 This gabion wall was built over a gravel driveway, so the ground was already compact and firm. If you are building a gabion wall at the back of a border, excavate the top 4–6 in. of soil and level it to create a firm base. Assemble the gabions by winding the helical wire coils along each edge, leaving one panel open for the lid. Set the gabions in position with their lids opening toward the face side of the wall and so that the helical coil on their corners overlaps. Then fix the gabions together by pushing locking pins (straight metal rods with a hooked end) down through the overlapping wire coil on the corners. Half-fill the face of the cages with stone, laying the stone in neat, tightly fitting courses.

2 The stone used in this project is green slate, which is relatively expensive. This is why it is only used to face the cages. Hidden behind it is a mixture of gravel, broken

MATERIALS

16 × 16 × 39½ in. gabions

39½-in. and 16-in. helical wire coils

16-in. locking pins

Slate

Gravel, broken bricks, or any type of ballast

Landscape fabric

16-in. metal ties

1 Once you have positioned the gabions and fixed them together, half-fill with stones, laying them neatly and as close together as possible.

2 To cut costs on materials, use the stone to face the gabion and shovel unwanted material, such as broken bricks, into sheets of landscape fabric.

KNOW YOUR MATERIALS

Gabions can be ordered direct from the manufacturer in any size. They are an ideal solution if you want walls and have a lot of material, such as stone or broken concrete, that you want to get rid of. The look is dependent on what the inside of the cages are filled with, and even they can be covered in wood. Another variation is to use soil as the infill behind the facing stone and plant saplings out through the mesh to soften the face of the stone. Although the sides of the gabions can be held together with wire ties, it is much more convenient to use helical wire coils. These are stronger and easier to wind into position, and unlike wire ties, they don't leave any sharp edges.

3 As each gabion is filled, secure the lid using helical wire coils and lock the gabions by bending over the ends of the wire coils.

bricks, and sand inside landscape fabric, which prevents the finer particles from escaping. Gabions can be filled with any stone or ballast, as long as it is frostproof and packed in firmly. When you've half-filled the gabion, brace the front and back of the cage with metal ties every four spaces to prevent the face of the gabion from bowing.

3 Fill the cages, firming the infill as you go. Then fold the landscape fabric over the top, close the lid, and seal it by winding the wire coils along its front edge and sides. Lock the gabions by bending down the ends of the wire coils (this also makes their sharp ends safe). Repeat the process, and then on the final course, cover the landscape fabric with a layer of stone so that it is hidden.

Planting

Pack soil between the courses of stones and plant drought-tolerant plants such as sedum (*Sedum*). (See pages 108–109 for details on watering.)

brick retaining WALL

This wall is easy on the eye and warm to the touch. It holds back the soil and nurtures the plants in its shelter. The curve leads up a flight of steps, while its top makes the ideal ad hoc seat for parties. Unfortunately, having a retaining wall built for you can be expensive. This project, combined with the information in the techniques section, tells you all you need to know to do it yourself and how to save money on materials.

1 Mark out and excavate the foundation for the wall using a line attached to a stake to score the arc of the wall. Then, pour the concrete into the foundation, allowing a gap of at least two courses between the top of the foundation and the soil level to make space for plants or paving. When you are building a wall into a bank, terrace the foundation to reduce the number of bricks needed to reach soil level. To build a flight of steps into the bank, you will need retaining walls to hold the soil from their sides, as well as along the face of the bank. To build a stepped foundation, peg a piece of wood overlapping the lower foundation by at least 18 in. The rise of the step must equal the height of the course (that is, one or two bricks plus their mortar joint), or it will be difficult to marry the wall above and below the step.

MATERIALS

Ballast and building sand

Chalk

Cement

Bricks

High-density concrete blocks

Brick ties

Bamboo stake

Imitation stone concrete paving slabs

TOOLS

Groundwork tools

Masonry and bricklaying tools

Wood mortar board

1 Smooth over the surface of the foundation using a trowel. Let it set for at least forty-eight hours before starting construction.

2 Lay blocks along the back face of the straight part of the wall, starting with the end blocks.

KNOW YOUR MATERIALS

To save time and money, concrete blocks can be used to build up the back of the wall, hidden behind stretcher bond face bricks. Concrete blocks and bricks are deliberately proportioned for use together, and a single course of concrete blocks is equal in height to three courses of bricks. When the two courses are at the same level (i.e., every three, six, nine bricks), the two can be joined with brick ties. These are galvanized S-shaped rods that are bedded into the mortar every 3 ft. along the wall. Alternately, build the out-of-sight part of the wall using "commons." These are bricks that have an uneven color and texture, and a low price tag.

2 Next mark the back face of the wall on the foundation using chalk, and lay high-density concrete blocks along this line on a ½-in. joint of 1:3 cement and soft sand mortar. At this stage, only work on the straight parts of the wall. As with any wall, always put the end blocks in position first and run a line between them, because this speeds up positioning the central blocks. Once they are tapped down to the line, use a level to check that they are vertical.

3 Mark the position of the front face of the wall with chalk. The width should be 8½ in., leaving a ½-in. gap between the two skins. Lay bricks to make the front skin, using a 1:3 mix for the bricks below ground and a 1:5 mix above ground. Again, build up the ends first and run a line by which to guide the bricks in the middle, checking levels as you go. Care must be taken to keep the joints even, or the third course of bricks won't correspond with the height of the concrete block. A jointing tool is a good gauge (see page 35).

4 When the third course is complete, point the face of the wall. At this stage, the bricks and blocks should be level. Spread the mortar for the next course of blocks, and press one end of a brick tie into it, jutting the other over the top of the bricks. Use one tie every 3 ft., and lay the next course of blocks on top.

5 Score the face of the curved wall on the foundation using a line attached to a bamboo stake. The curve consists of header bricks and bricks cut into wedges, laid alternately. To cut the bricks, mark a wedge-shaped line around the brick, set it on a bed of sand, and strike around the line with a chisel until it breaks along the line. If you find that the bricks keep shattering, it may be because your chisel isn't sharp enough. If necessary, you can use a half-brick for the front and one-fourth of a brick behind it instead.

6 Stagger the joints of each course, using a level bridged between the ends of the straight sections of the wall as a height guide. Cut bricks as necessary to match into the

3 Build the first three courses of the brick face of the wall, starting with the ends and using a line as a leveling guide.

4 Lay the second course of blocks, using brick ties to join the concrete blocks and the bricks together.

5 Next lay the curved part of the wall, alternately using headers and bricks cut into wedge shapes.

straight sections and check that the face of the wall is vertical as you go.

7 Once the curved section is three courses high, lay bricks along the straight sections of the wall over the brick ties. Then repeat Steps 5 and 6 until the wall is six courses high, pointing the joints before the mortar dries.

8 Spread mortar over the second course of blocks and press brick ties into it as before, but lay two courses of bricks over the top instead of a block to give the illusion that the wall is completely made of brick when viewed from the back. Lay the front two courses, point, and allow to dry. Line the back of the wall and lay drainage (see page 23); backfill up to the level of the top two bricks. Set the coping stones on a 1:3 mix, making them level.

Practice makes perfect

Read the information on pages 24 and 25 to help you design a wall that looks good, but that is also structurally sound. Before starting work, spend a little time practicing the basic techniques, such as buttering and laying bricks to level (see page 24). You don't have to build a wall or waste materials to do this; simply mix a bucket of 1:10 mortar and building sand that is strong enough to be sticky but can easily be broken apart again once you've mastered the basics.

Construction tips

Until you get up to speed, only mix a small quantity of mortar at a time to prevent waste. If the weather is hot, keep the mortar covered to prevent it from drying out too quickly. Before you start laying, give the foundation a sprinkle of water to keep the mortar soft while you get your first levels. Point the joints and scrape any mortar off the face of the wall before covering with plastic and leaving overnight. Cover the unused stacks of bricks and blocks as well, as they are easier to butter when dry. On subsequent days, dampen the top of the wall before building to keep it moist while you tap the bricks level.

6 As you build, stagger the joints between the courses and check that the wall is vertical and level across its top.

7 Point the joints between the brickwork as the mortar stiffens, and continue to build up the height of the wall.

8 Allow the wall to dry for twenty-four hours. Then set the coping stones on top, filling the joints between them with mortar.

fences

planning fences

Fences have an important function—demarcation—but they don't need to be boring. Not only are there lots of different types of fences, but there are also many variations in style that each can adopt. Wood is the most common type of garden boundary. It is versatile, weathers well, and looks natural in a garden setting. Whether made from panels or slats of wood, it creates a neat, rhythmical line that complements the softer, less formal shape of borders.

Function and style Wood has been used in gardens for thousands of years because it is easy to work with, long-lasting, and it integrates with the garden as it ages. Depending on the type of fence, wood lends itself to large perimeter boundaries or lighter internal divides. Truly adaptable, it can be a defense against trespassers, an enclosure to keep children or pets in, or an inviting front yard picket that beckons visitors to enter.

The main choice is whether to make fences from scratch—cutting wood posts and planks exactly to your own design—or to buy in simpler panel form. There are advantages to each—a homemade version will be perfectly customized to your garden and taste, whereas panel fences are quicker and simpler to erect.

The style is often dictated by construction methods—for example, whether you are using metal brackets or linking the wood with more rustic interlocking mortise joints. The more craft that goes into the fence, the more beautiful it will be. If you are looking for an opportunity for creativity, go for a picket fence. There are infinite possibilities for the shape of the uprights, from Gothic points to arrowheads, as well as any new design of your own.

Design choices One of the first questions you should ask is whether the fence is to be a physical enclosure—so that you can see through it or over it, but it stops you in your tracks—or a visual enclosure, creating a total screen from the outside world. For example, a picket fence offers physical enclosure without blocking views or lowering light levels, unlike a privacy fence.

In a countryside setting, there are often opportunities for incorporating the surrounding landscape into the garden, in which case you want a fence that subtly demarcates your

A wood pole divide.

Privacy fence with rail caps.

Living willow fence.

Rustic pole fence.

Climbing plants can really spruce up a fence (top left), their foliage blending the wood with the garden. If it is contrast you're after, paint effects, such as black wood stain with acid green paint (top right), make a zingy color combination. For decoration (above), an arrowhead picket fence combined with an ornamental arch creates a facade with style.

Heavy oak post-and-rail fences are charming and long-lasting—useful for both perimeter and internal divides.

land without detracting from the view. A post-and-rail fence is not only see-through, but the hewn rails appear as if they have just been cut from the surrounding trees. On the other hand, in an exposed area or a rural setting, you may want a boundary that makes you feel safe and says "keep out" while also providing seclusion, and the best option for this is a privacy fence.

Both fences could work well in a city or suburban environment, but in the country there are more opportunities for modern twists with wood stains or claddings. Wood boundaries will always be in vogue because of the way they can be continuously updated, either with a fresh coat of paint or by tying it in with a deck for a modern look. Dripping with climbing plants and allowed to bleach in the sun, fences can look old-fashioned; planed and painted, they have a modern look.

Types of fencing

Panel—This is probably the most ubiquitous type of fence. Typically sold in 6 x 6 ft. units, they are inexpensive and fairly simple to construct, because they go up in 6-ft. chunks and are held in the ground by fence posts on either side. The more you pay, the better the wood, the construction, and the detailing of the panel.

Lower-end larch panels tend to become warped over time and really need to be clothed and hidden by plants. You have a choice of wood or concrete gravel boards and posts.

Shadow box—When viewed straight on, this double-faced fence appears solid; when looked at from the side, though, you'll notice it has gaps to allow the breeze to filter through, making it ideal for a windy, exposed site.

Post-and-rail—This is a very simple enclosure. Depending on the wood used and the finish, it can have a modern or country look. It can be charming when the flower heads of low perennials poke through the gaps.

Privacy—The effect is like a well-made panel fence, but in fact, this type of fence is constructed from individual planks of wood nailed to a post-and-rail frame. Because it's made from separate planks, it's easy to modify—to avoid the branches of a tree or to follow curved or sloping ground, for example. Like a panel fence, it is easily painted and embellished with decorative finials and capping rails.

Picket—These have loads of charm, because they are architectural enough to pick up details in houses, but open and airy enough to allow plants to grow through. Most often used for front yards, they are underused as internal divides, such as around a vegetable patch.

The downside of solid fences is that they block out light, making the conditions on the sheltered side cold and shady. Where possible, it is much better to use fences with gaps between their beams, such as this hit and miss palisade (above left) or diamond-crossed fencing (above right). In good growing conditions, plants will happily fill the gaps and even billow through their sides.

Arrowhead picket.

Hexagon picket.

Chestnut pole palisade.

Wattle fence.

post-and-rail FENCE

A split chestnut post-and-rail fence creates a rustic-looking divide that harmonizes with meadow areas, cottages, and prairie-style gardens. The twisted, honey-colored wood makes a see-through frame for borders in winter that gradually fills with flowering plants through the summer.

1 The height of the posts and the length of the rails depend on the location of the boundary. In a large garden, cutting down the posts and rails isn't necessary. However, in most gardens, it is a good idea to cut down the posts and rails into 4-ft. lengths, using a hand saw, to produce a scaled-down version. To mark the positions of the rails on the fence posts, mock up the fence flat on the ground, moving the rails up and down until they look right. I made the center of the rails 6½ in. and 20 in. down from the top of the fence post. Make the joints for the rails about 3 in. long and 1 in. wide, drilling out as much wood as possible before chiseling them square.

2 Cut the rails to length if necessary and sharpen their ends using an ax or billhook—resting them over a block of wood or a tree stump is the easiest way to do this. Overlap the ends inside the fence posts, making

MATERIALS

6-ft. chestnut posts

TOOLS

Carpentry tools

Masonry and bricklaying tools

Ax or billhook

Drill

1 Make mortise joints in the posts by first drilling out as much wood as possible and then removing the rest with a chisel.

2 Once the rails have been cut to length, rest them on a block of wood or a tree stump and use an ax or billhook to sharpen their ends.

KNOW YOUR MATERIALS

Chestnut fence spikes are most commonly used as supports for economical temporary cordon fences around building sites, but it is as post-and-rail fences that chestnut excels. This is due to the twisted and curved nature of the wood, which creates a boundary with a soft, wavy outline. They are available in 6-ft. lengths from building supply stores. When you buy, handpick the lengths yourself, choosing the widest planks for the posts and narrower lengths for the rails. Alternately, buy premortised square 30-in. posts to create a more formal fence.

3 *Use a sledgehammer to drive the posts into the ground, having hooked the rails between pairs of posts.*

what's called a "scarf joint." This gives the rail a neat finish—especially if you sharpen the opposite sides of each end, as shown here. Also sharpen the ends of the posts into points.

3   Use a sledgehammer to drive the first post into the ground, checking by eye that it is upright. Position another post and hook rails between the two. They don't need to be tight because they will be pushed into the joints as you hammer the second post into the ground. Repeat the process right along the fence run. An option at each end is to attach two rails, angling them down from the fence into the soil to give extra support.

Chestnut posts have a remarkable ability to resist the weather and won't rot in above-ground positions for decades. However, it is wise to give the posts extra protection. The best way of doing this is to dip their bases in wood preservative before hammering them into the ground.

post-and-panel FENCE

Painted in gentle, hazy blue, this line of dome-topped panel fencing makes the perfect backdrop to a seaside garden. Its straight, crisp lines echo those of the deck and contrast beautifully with the pebbles and large tropical palms.

1 Most fence panels have been treated with a wood preservative during the manufacturing process, however, because the colors are often so sallow, you'll want to paint them anyway. It is a good idea to do this before you build the fence, as it is easier to get into nooks and crannies on both sides without having to step on your own—or your neighbors'—borders. It also allows you to catch the drips of paint that run from one side of the fence to the other.

2 Run a taut string along the ground to mark out the front of the fence, and level out any undulations in the ground. This is necessary because panel fences, particularly those with domed or concave tops, look best when they are all level. If you are building your fence on a slope and have a slight rise along your fence line, you can raise the height of the fence at the bottom of the slope by fixing an

1 Start by painting the panels before erecting them, so that you can get into all the nooks and crannies with ease.

2 Having marked out the front of the fence and leveled the ground, hammer in the first fence spike, making sure it is upright.

KNOW YOUR MATERIALS

There are hundreds of different styles of panel fences, ranging from the ubiquitous larch to bamboo to willow panels held in a wood frame. The rule is that the more you pay, the more robust the panels will be and the more thought and time will have gone into their detailing and design. The panels used in this project are made up of two lines of overlapping boards with a ³⁄₈-in. gap between them. The gap is small enough to maintain privacy, but large enough to allow air to filter through the fence, reducing turbulence on the sheltered side and buffeting when wind speeds are high (for more information, see page 10). Alternately, use square or concave-topped panels.

extra gravel board beneath it, while setting the gravel board into the soil at the top. As well as extra gravel boards, you'll need longer fence posts for the downslope end of the fence. Starting at one end of the run, hammer in the first fence spike, ensuring that it is upright and parallel with the line (see page 19 for extra details).

3 Put the first post into the top of the spike, using a level to ensure that the post is upright as you tighten the bolts. To find the position of the next post spike, either get someone to prop the panel against the first post, or lay the panel flat on the ground, using its base as a guide. Because the widths of the panels vary, it is always best to measure the distance between posts with the panel that will go between them. Then hammer the next fence spike into the ground. Repeat Steps 1, 2, and 3 until the fence has reached the required length.

4 To keep from having to perform the awkward, time-consuming job of sawing the post tops level after the fence is built, use a straightedged plank to bridge between the top of each fence spike and check their heights with a level. If they are different, tap them down with a sledgehammer, then insert the fence post.

5 Gravel boards sit below the fence panels, preventing them from coming into contact with the soil and thereby keeping the base of the fence panels from rotting. They also allow you to pile soil against the base of the fence to fill any hollows and even out the soil level. Because they are in contact with the soil, they will rot first, so they should always be fixed separately to the panel to allow for easy replacement. Do this by centering each gravel board between the fence spikes and hammering three 15-in. treated wood pegs into the ground alongside the board.

6 Using a drill, fix the gravel board to the post with two screws. As you work along the row, check that each board is fixed at the same height with a level or by

3 Lay the panel flat on the ground, using it as a base guide. Then hammer the next fence spike into the ground.

4 Rest a straightedged plank between the top of each fence spike and check that they are level. Tap them down if necessary.

5 To fix gravel boards to the bottom of the fence, first hammer a treated wood peg into the ground beside the fence spike.

running a taut string line between the two end posts to mark their height.

7 Fix panels in place by resting them on top of the gravel boards and screwing diagonally through their sides into the posts. Use three screws spaced evenly down the side of each panel, drilling their pilot holes first. Then to protect the tops of the post from the weather, nail fence caps to the tops of the posts.

8 Till the soil in the border in front of the fence, adding extra soil and compost to conceal the metal spikes before planting.

Disguising fence spikes

Because metal fence spikes don't absorb paint as well as the wood in a fence, they are difficult to disguise. The way around this problem is either to plant an evergreen shrub or perennial in front of the spikes or to bury the spikes beneath the soil. The burying technique works best when the soil on both sides of the fence is raised, or excavated and backfilled after the fence is built.

Replacing broken fence posts

The weakest part of a panel fence and the most likely to succumb to rot is where the fence posts come into contact with the soil. It is at this point that the fence will break during strong winds, causing it to lean or even fall over.

When fence spikes have been used, a broken post is easily unbolted and replaced, but where posts are concreted in, replacing them is more problematic. This is because it is almost impossible to pull the broken stump out from the concrete footing.

By far the easiest option is to cut off the post at ground level and use a repair spike—these are similar to the fence spikes used in this project, but with a shorter point. The spike is driven between the remains of the rotten post and the concrete that surrounds it, and provides a socket to hold the replacement post.

6 Having checked that each gravel board is at the same height, screw the board to the post using a drill.

7 Next fix the painted panels by resting them on top of the gravel boards and screwing diagonally into the posts.

8 Finally, till the soil in front of your fence, adding extra soil and compost to hide the metal spikes before planting.

privacy fence with POST CAPS

This privacy fence combines elegant, regimented lines with the strength and rhythm created by the repeated overlapping boards and stringers. Structurally, it is very strong, and it will bear the weight of large climbers and trained fruit trees.

1 The ends of each stringer have a notch of wood removed from them that corresponds to a similar notch cut in the posts, creating a notch joint. This joint gives the fence extra strength and brings the face of the stringers in line with the face of the posts, so that the tapered boards form one continuous line running the length of the fence. To create the notch in the stringers, lay them with their widest face down and make a saw cut 2 in. from the ends and ¾ in. deep. Then starting from the end of the stringer, chisel back to the saw cut, removing the uppermost triangle of wood. Chiseling can be made easier and more accurate by making two or three extra saw cuts in from the end.

2 To make the notch in the fence posts, first mark in pencil the tops and bottoms of the stringers. The top rail should be 12 in. from the top of the post, and the bottom rail

MATERIALS

Triangular stringers

4-in.-wide posts and
8-ft.-long tapered boards

3-in. galvanized nails

Cement and hardcore

6-in. gravel boards

2-in. nails

Post caps and cover strips

TOOLS

Carpentry tools

Groundwork tools

Masonry and bricklaying tools

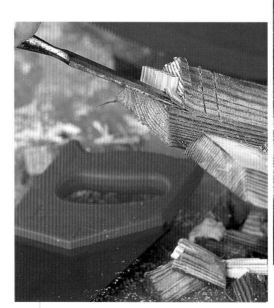

1 Once you have made a saw cut in the stringer, chisel back to the cut, removing the uppermost triangle of wood.

2 After marking the tops and bottoms of the stringers onto the post and using a circular saw to cut along the lines, chisel out the wood.

KNOW YOUR MATERIALS

This privacy fence consists of tapered boards nailed to horizontal lengths of wood called "stringers," which in turn are fixed to fence posts. Because all of the components fit together like a puzzle, the height of the fence and the distribution of the fence posts can be tweaked to avoid obstacles such as tree roots and branches, or to enclose difficult spaces. Usually, though, the posts are set at 8-ft. centers because the stringers are sold in 16-ft. lengths, and cutting them in half makes them easy to handle and avoids waste. There are two types of stringers: triangular (used here) and square with a beveled top. Of the two, the triangular shape has more graceful lines.

should be 5 ft. 5 in. from the top, and the middle rail equidistant between the two. The quickest way to cut out the notches is to lay the posts in line on a flat surface (to level up uneven ground, lay down two lengths of wood first, and sit the posts on these). Use a circular saw, with the blade angled at 45° and set to a depth of ¾ in., to cut along the lines, marking the top and bottom of the stringers. Be sure that the blade is angled toward the center of the rail, otherwise the joints will be the wrong shape. Then chisel out between the saw cuts.

3 Dig holes 24 in. deep for the end posts and prop into position, holding them firmly with wooden stakes driven into the ground. Then run two string lines along the faces of the posts, one at the top and one at the bottom. Mark the position of intermediate fence posts using a stringer as a spacing guide, and dig out 24-in. holes for these. Place a post in each hole and check that it is wide enough to allow the post to touch the string lines; also check that the hole is at the correct depth.

4 Starting at one end and working on one post at a time, fix the bottom stringer onto the post with a 3-in. nail to ensure the correct spacing. Move the post so that its face comes up to the string lines. Use a level to check that the post is upright and at the correct height. Prop it in position with hardcore and backfill around the post with concrete. Once all the posts are in place, check them for position and level, and adjust if necessary, then allow the concrete to set for at least twenty four hours.

5 Use 3-in. nails to fix the remaining stringers to the posts. Because the concrete won't be fully hardened, support the back of each post with a length of sturdy wood while you hammer. Better yet, get someone to hold the post steady for you.

6 The position of the gravel board is 2 in. below the bottom stringer. Mark this position with a line on each post, and nail the gravel boards just below it. Any dips or lumps in the soil can be leveled later on.

3 When you have put the posts in the holes, run a line between their tops and bottoms to check that they are positioned correctly.

4 Once you have fixed the bottom stringer onto the post and put the post in the correct position, backfill with concrete.

5 When fixing the rails to the posts, make sure the back of the post is supported by a piece of wood.

7 | All wood expands and contracts as the temperature and moisture content of the air fluctuates. To allow for this movement, the tapered boards overlap each other by $^3/_4$ in. To keep from having to measure this overlap for each board, make a spacer from a length of batten cut to the width of the boards with a nail hammered through it $^3/_4$ in. from the end. Rest each tapered board on the gravel board, check that it is level, and fix it in place with 2-in. nails—one in each stringer. Then using the spacer, position and fix the following board.

8 | Nail post caps on the fence posts and cover strips over the tapered boards to protect their end grain from the weather.

To make the strips fit snugly around the boards, cut notches that are $^1/_2$ in. deep and 4 in. long where the posts occur. Place into position and sit on top of the fence and nail onto the thickest part of the tapered board and the posts.

Tip

It's always easier to build a fence with two people to set out posts: one person holding them in position and another checking for line and level.

Design choices

If you want to avoid the work of chiseling joints where the stringers and fence posts meet, you can simply screw the rails to the face of the posts. You have to use square, rather than triangular, stringers, and although this is a quicker method, the finished fence will be wider and not as strong. If, on the other hand, the idea of woodwork sets your pulse racing, building a fence with stringers mortised into the posts will be right up your alley. The method of doing this is similar to building a post-and-rail fence (see pages 64–65). Chisel holes through the posts at the height of each stringer and sharpen the rails so they fit snugly inside. Then nail the tapered boards in place. The posts are visible from both sides, making for a very smart and narrow boundary.

6 Once the stringers are in place, nail a gravel board to each post, leaving a 2-in. gap between the board and the ground.

7 Having nailed the first tapered board to the stringer, use a spacer to position the next board.

8 Finally, nail post caps onto the tops of the fence posts and cover strips onto the thickest part of the tapered boards.

picket FENCE

A walk down any country lane will take you past cottages surrounded by charming picket fences, with climbers spun through the top and flowers poking their heads between the palisade. The look never grows old, because picket has such great potential for whimsical detail that accentuates the personality of its home and owner.

MATERIALS

$^3/_4$ x $2^1/_2$ in. planed wood for the pickets

Paint

3-in. fence posts

Concrete

Batten braces

Screws

Treated wood

$^2/_3$ x $2^1/_2$ in. planed wood for the rails

Height gauge and spacer

Decorative caps

TOOLS

Jigsaw

Surform or electric sander

Sandpaper

Level

Hand saw

Drill

1   Sketch out designs for the pickets that will complement your house. When you've decided which is the most appropriate, make a template from a scrap piece of wood. As well as the shape of the top, consider the size of the gap between them and decide how far apart the pickets need to be in order to look their best. If the space is wider than the width of the wood, it will look gappy. Modify your design until it looks good, with a space somewhere between two-thirds and the full width of the wood.

2   Cut the wood for the pickets to length. This should be the desired height of the fence less 2 in., so the bases of the pickets are clear of the soil and away from rot. Draw around the template on the end of each picket and cut to shape using a jigsaw. To save time, clamp two pickets at a time to a workbench.

1 When you have chosen a design for your pickets, use a jigsaw to make a template from a scrap piece of wood.

2 Having drawn around the template on each picket, clamp two at a time to a workbench and cut to shape.

CHOOSING A DESIGN

It's worth taking the time to assess the height of your fence. Too small, and it can look insignificant; too high, and its elegance is lost. Between $19\frac{1}{2}$ and $39\frac{1}{2}$ in. is ideal, depending on the size of the garden it encloses. As for the tops of the pickets, take your cue for the shape from the location, such as the house, the greenhouse, or the shapes of distant roofs. The wood for this fence was cut into tulip shapes, echoing the curved lines of the thatch roof on the cottage it surrounds and as a tribute to the owner's passion for flowers. Think about the shape of the gaps between the boards, as well. Here they make wine goblet shapes—a celebratory touch.

3 | Smooth the edges of the pickets with an electric sander or surform. This gives the fence a softer look and makes painting easier. The tops can be done with sandpaper or with a grinder fitted with a sanding disk.

4 | Picket fences are difficult to paint because they have so many crooks and crevices. To save time and trouble, give the sides of the pickets a coat of paint all at once. Do this by bunching them on their edges on a table, painting, and then tilting them over to keep the paint from gathering and gluing them together. Once they are dry, turn them over and paint the edge on the other side. The color of paint should, like the design, match the surroundings. Off-white is traditional, because it matches well with the window frames of most houses.

5 | Dig holes for the end and corner fence posts (these need to be at least a third of the height of the fence), and set the posts in concrete, propped in an upright position. To keep posts from moving during construction, hammer a batten diagonally into the soil beside each post and screw it to the side of the post. Where the fence attaches to a wall, as it does here, screw a length of 2 × 4 in. treated wood directly to the wall (for gates, see below). Dig out holes for the intermediate posts, which should be no more than 6 ft. apart, because the wood for the rails is fairly light. Screw the lower rail in position between the end and corner posts—the height from the ground depends on how tall your fence is and what you think will look best, but somewhere between 2 and 6 in. is typical. Lower the intermediate fence posts into their holes using the rail as a positioning guide. Use a level to check that they are upright and straight, and then screw the rail to their side and fill the hole with concrete.

6 | Allow the concrete to dry for at least twenty-four hours and then attach the top rail. The height, as for the lower rail, depends on how tall your fence is and the shape of its top. As a general rule, make the space between the top and bottom similar for traditional pointed-top

3 To give the fence a softer look, use a surform or an electric sander to remove the rough edges.

4 Next, lay the pickets together on a table and, to save time, paint their edges all at once rather than individually.

5 Having dug the holes and dropped in the posts, use a level to check that they are upright before filling with concrete.

designs, and bigger at the top to show off more elaborate designs. Before attaching the pickets, paint both rails to save time later. To locate the position of the pickets, cut a height gauge from a piece of wood to rest on the top rail, with a spacer to judge the gap between them. Check with a level before screwing from the back of the fence (so the screws won't show).

7 Remove the batten braces from the fence posts after forty eight hours, and using a hand saw, cut the post tops to level. Add decorative caps to protect them from the weather. There are two types of caps widely available: one in the shape of a ball and the other an acorn. Choose the one that fits most closely with the design of your pickets.

8 For a neat finish, hide the screw holes with a weatherproof filler, sanding it flush when it is dry, then paint the faces and backs of the pickets.

Design tips for including gates

If your picket fence includes a gate, this needs to be at a comfortable height to open, regardless of the height of the picket. The concave design shown here highlights the gate's position, and its lazily bowing top gives it a relaxed, informal look. Also, a concave top works best where the gap between the gate posts is wider than the height of the fence. However, to create a more formal look, go for a domed top, because it is taller and more imposing.

Another clue to the gate's position is its visible posts, which have rails mortised into their sides (see "Using wood," pages 26–27). It is a little more work, but it is worth doing because it gives a tidy finish, adds extra detail, and allows the gate to be hung in line with the fence.

The fixings you choose depend on the style of the gate. In this case, long, black, iron hinges instead of a latch and a gate spring were used, which gently pushes it shut behind you. As there is no latch, screw a gate stop made from a thin strip of wood to the inside of the post to prevent the spring from closing the gate beyond the line of the fence.

6 Before screwing the pickets onto the rails, use a level to check that they are completely straight.

7 Once the pickets are in place, use a hand saw to cut the post tops level with the pickets.

8 Finally, paint the faces and backs of the pickets and the rails if they weren't painted at an earlier stage.

trellises, screens, and claddings

planning trellises, screens, and claddings

This chapter is devoted to masquerade—hiding the reality of ugly boundaries with dramatic embellishments, while increasing your privacy in the process. Suggestive of outdoor living, the materials are influenced by trends in interior design, which rely on the beauty of individual materials and how well they blend in with a natural setting. Their appeal derives as much from the components as from the way the light plays through and across their surfaces.

Function and style While the theme of creating privacy and enclosure persists, these trellises, claddings, and screens have various functions. Glass gives an open, airy feel to a space and is particularly suited to small, already-enclosed gardens. It can be used as a detail within a trellis or as the screen itself. The only type of glass to use is toughened and sandblasted, because it is opaque, therefore, it is not a danger to birds, and, of course, it is very strong. It's a dynamic material that reflects its surroundings and becomes more transparent in rain. At night, in the beam of a spotlight, it glows and diffuses the light.

The best trellis has not forgotten its classical heritage, reminiscent of Roman colonnades and medieval cloisters. Sadly, all too often it doesn't live up to its promise due to cheap construction and unimaginative use. When made well, a custom-made trellis can give a romantic otherworldliness to an existing wall, and offers exciting opportunities for climbing plants and nighttime lighting.

For a more instant transformation, you can't beat cladding, such as that made from natural stems like split bamboo. Wired together on rolls, the bamboo can disguise an unappealing fence or enhance a theme, like a Japanese garden. It is economical and certainly much cheaper than replacing a whole fence. More sophisticated metal claddings, like copper and stainless steel, aren't for such wholesale use. Instead, they can be used as focal points, giving an ordinary boundary an artistic twist.

Temporary screens, like the summer structures that support sweet peas (*Lathyrus odoratus*) and scarlet runners (*Phaseolus coccineus*), are playful and seasonal. By replacing traditional materials such as bamboo stakes with hazelwood, a plant support screen will last for several years. It is also a fantastic way of creating instant rooms while

Living willow lattice.

Woven willow screen.

Painted trellis.

Custom heavy wood trellis.

The metal-clad walls (top left and right) are surprisingly dynamic. Stainless steel reflects the shapes and colors in the garden that surrounds it, while mild steel turns every shade of coral and cinnamon as it rusts. Both are modern and uncompromising in effect and are tricky to work with. In complete contrast, bamboo screens (above) are much simpler to construct and change little as they age.

Each type of woven wall has its own unique character. Hazelwood screens are solid in appearance and are suitable for perimeter and internal boundaries.

waiting for permanent hedges to grow. Longer-lasting are rusty metal screens, which have an urban feel and introduce spicy colors in an elemental way.

Design choices Glass and metal should be integrated with the surroundings; this is best achieved by giving them a function, such as masking an unattractive feature or leading the eye to an entrance. Both need an anchor, such as an appropriately modern material at their base or plants that ground them, making them seem like they belong. Metal claddings can be used very subtly (for example, to adorn window boxes). This approach works well because it links claddings on walls to other areas of the garden, making the decision to use the material less arbitrary. Similarly, with more traditional screens like wood trellises, linking them to other parts of the garden gives them reason. So, if it's painted, repeat the color on woodwork elsewhere, such as on fence posts.

Types of trellises, screens, and claddings Glass is expensive because it must be cut to size and toughened before it is delivered. On the positive side, all you have to do is fix it in position, so it's installed quickly. Sandblasted

glass has two faces: a smooth side and the side that has been treated. For reflections, have the smooth side facing out. For a softer finish, display the other.

You can buy trellises for adding instant height to existing boundaries, for jazzing up walls and fences, and for giving body to freestanding arbors and pergolas. Custom trellises can be constructed to fit any space without any of the ugly seams that detract from store-bought panels.

The various types of cladding include bamboo, tree heather, peeled reed, and willow, each bestowing a garden with a different character. Bamboo obviously enhances an Asian theme, but it can also look quite jungle-like. Tree heather gives a Mediterranean feel, and peeled reeds and willows are suited to a cottage garden.

There are two main choices with stems—either to buy a dead stem that won't regrow, or a living stem, like willow, that will sprout and turn into a living screen. Hazelwood is more reluctant to root, and bamboo stakes, of course, cannot be expected to grow.

Metal is available in sheet form or grate, and the latter is good for giving a modern twist on trellises. Copper and steel are sold by the sheet and can be worked at home with a jigsaw fitted with a metal blade; stainless steel, on the other hand, is hard to cut, so it should be made to order.

Trellises can be a work of art in their own right. The cladding in the style of a Mondrian painting has stained glass fixed between the bars, adding extra color and interest (above left). In contrast, the combination of industrial materials, such as stainless steel floor tiles and corrugated steel sheets, in a garden setting (above right) shakes off their municipal associations.

Trellis as balustrade.

Willow in a Japanese-style lattice.

Light, airy, wood trellis.

A stem of jasmine climbs around the trellis.

glass SCREEN

Using glass in a garden is like bringing the indoors outside. It always looks very modern, whether combined with structural plants like flax (*Phormium*) and palms or with cottage-garden flowers. It's the ideal material for built-up areas because it creates privacy without reducing light levels.

1 | This project involves combining custom ready-made materials to make a screen that's unique. Decide on the measurements and number of glass panels, and order frames made from 1½-in. boxed steel to hold the panels from a blacksmith, garage, or metal workshop. These should be H-shaped and wide enough to fit the glass and the clamps, plus an extra ⅛ in. to make fixing the glass easier. The legs need to be at least 27½ in. long to provide a deep concrete footing.

Paint the underground section of the frame with rustproof paint. Put the legs in 24-in. holes in the ground and pour a 1:5 cement and ballast mix around them. Tamp the concrete with a length of wood to remove any air bubbles, and slope its surface with a trowel to shed water away from the metal. Check for level and prop in place with wood while the concrete dries.

MATERIALS

H-shaped metal frame made from 1½-in. boxed steel—this one is 7 ft. tall and just over 4 ft. wide

Metal paint and rust proofer

Ballast

Cement

Eight metal clamps with a brushed finish

Self-tapping screws

Toughened and sandblasted ¼-in. glass— this one is 4 × 5 ft.

TOOLS

Masonry and bricklaying tools

Drill

Allen wrenches (to tighten clamps)

1 Having put the legs of the frame in holes, infill with concrete and check for level. Prop in place with wood while the concrete dries.

2 Once the frame is in position, paint the upper part and then attach the metal clamps to it, using self-tapping screws.

3 Lift the glass into position, resting its base on rubber stops placed on the bottom clamps. Next, fit the backs on the clamps and tighten.

2 | After forty-eight hours, remove the wood supports and paint the upper part of the frame. Then drill evenly spaced holes for the metal clamps, which are fixed to the frame with self-tapping screws. Self-tapping screws work by cutting their own thread as they are tightened into the metal. They are simple to use, as long as the hole they are wound into is just the right size. Either experiment with different bits on scraps of metal or buy a bit to match the screws. The clamps are made of aluminum and hold the glass in place between rubber jaws. To hold a 4 × 5 ft. sheet of glass, you'll need eight clamps: two for the base and three up each side.

3 | Lift the glass into position (this is a two-person job), resting its base on rubber stops placed on the bottom clamps. Fit the backs on the clamps and tighten. To prevent rainwater from getting inside the open tops of the metal frame, plug with rubber stops. And to stop unsightly mud splashes in wet weather, plant evergreens at the base or mulch with gravel.

store-bought TRELLISES

A trellis is more than a support for climbing plants. With a little imagination, it can be transformed into a focal point that captures the sun and shadows by day and illuminates the garden by night.

1 | Painting trellises by hand is a slow and laborious business, because the surface area of each panel is vast and because the wood almost always completely absorbs the first coat. It is more efficient to rent a handheld paint sprayer, which will do the job in minutes without leaving unsightly drips on the wood. Always choose a dry, windless day. To use a sprayer, water down the paint by a third, prop the trellis against a plastic sheet to catch any drips, and spray evenly across each panel, paying attention to the recesses around the frame. Allow the paint to dry for fifteen minutes and apply another coat. When you have finished, fill the container with warm water, and spray to clean the nozzle.

2 | To make the trellis pillars, screw together the 1-ft. panels into three-sided boxes using L-shaped metal brackets to hold their corners together.

MATERIALS

Nine 1 x 6 ft.
diamond trellis panels

Two 3 x 6 ft.
square panels

Water-soluble paint

Plastic sheeting

Twelve L-shaped metal brackets

Twelve flat metal fixing plates

Plastic screw anchors

Three low-voltage uplights

TOOLS

Rental tools

Level

Drill

1 Having watered down the paint by a third, rest the trellis against the plastic sheeting and use a handheld sprayer to paint the trellis.

2 Make the trellis pillars by screwing together the 1-ft. panels into three-sided boxes, using L-shaped brackets at the corners.

To look good, a trellis needs to be well made with straight beams and evenly proportioned squares. Often, a store-bought trellis falls short of these standards, and although it might seem like a bargain, it never lives up to its full potential. The things that separate the good from the bad are the quality of the wood, the hole size, and the design. So make sure that the finish of the wood is even and not a patchy mix of rough and smooth wood. Holes bigger than 5 in. are too large and will always look out of scale. If you're using a trellis structurally—for making pillars for lighting, for example—always opt for trellis panels with a framed edge, as this increases their strength.

3 Screw flat metal fixing plates to the back of the trellis pillars and screw them to the wall. Use a level to check that they are upright.

3 | Screw flat metal fixing plates to the back of the trellis pillars. Screw them to the wall as shown, checking with a level to ensure that each pillar is upright. To fix the trellis infills between the pillars, position them against the wall and drill through them to mark the plaster or brickwork below. Then remove the trellis, drill holes in the wall, and insert plastic screw anchors before placing the trellis back in position and fixing with screws.

Installing lighting

For lighting, use three low-voltage uplights bolted to the floor at the base of each pillar. Low-voltage lights consist of a transformer that steps down the voltage from the main electricity supply to just twelve volts, meaning that even if the wires were accidentally cut, there would be less risk of electrocution. Available as kits, you don't need a professional electrician to install them; simply position the transformer near a power socket indoors and run the wire to the lights along the base of the wall. This way, the wires are hidden when the trellis is screwed in place.

custom-made TRELLISES

A custom trellis enables you to create an illusion of opulence and grandeur without breaking the bank. By making your own trellis, you can tailor it to your garden precisely, transforming run-of-the-mill walls into classical colonnades and arches.

1 The size of the wood trellis depends on the situation. In this project, $^1/_4 \times {}^3/_4$ in. planed batten was used, because the finished trellis was situated in a yard only 16 ft. square—anything bigger would have looked out of place. If you are cladding a large expanse of wall that's visible from farther away, use a larger wood, such as $^3/_4 \times 1$ in. batten. Either buy it planed or save money by removing the rough edges yourself with an electric plane. You don't need to buy treated wood, as long as the base of the trellis is above soil level and you paint it with a protective wood stain. The first thing to do when building a custom trellis is to make your uprights by cutting twelve equal lengths of batten about 5 ft. long.

2 Cut the horizontal beams, making them 6 in. long, and nail them to the uprights using one of the horizontals as a spacing guide to ensure that the squares are even.

MATERIALS

180 ft. of planed
$^1/_4 \times {}^3/_4$ in. batten

$^5/_8$-in. copper tacks

4 × 8 ft. sheet of
$^1/_2$-in. marine plywood

Protective wood stain

Plastic screw anchors

2-in. screws

TOOLS

Carpentry tools

Bricklaying tools

Electric plane

Hammer

Drill with masonry bit

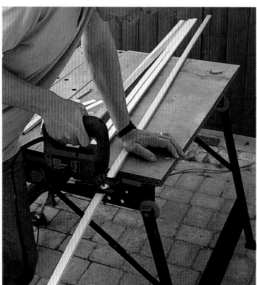

1 Start by making your uprights by cutting twelve equal lengths of batten approximately 5 ft. long.

2 Cut the horizontal beams, making them 6 in. long, and nail them to the uprights using one of the beams as a spacing guide.

KNOW YOUR MATERIALS

Combining squares and diamonds gives the trellis a three-dimensional appearance. The square sections look heavy and recessed compared with the diamond panels. For this reason, they look best when used as pillars or as infill between them. Always separate the two patterns with lengths of batten or plinths (as done here) to create the impression that one sits behind or atop the other. Another trick for creating a 3-D effect is to sandwich the horizontal and diamond beams between a double frame (see Step 2). This means that they are held away from the wall, which creates shadows to play behind them, producing an illusion of depth.

When you reach the height you want, cut the tops of the uprights flush with the last horizontal. Then sandwich the horizontals between another upright nailed over their top.

3 On top of the uprights, plinths add extra detail and separate the square from the diamond trellis. To make them, screw two rectangles of ½-in. marine plywood together, as shown—the larger rectangle is 3 x 9½ in., and the smaller rectangle is 2½ x 8 in. If you use a jigsaw, sand their edges to remove any splinters. Then pilot and screw them to the top of the uprights.

4 Each arch is made up of four semicircles of marine plywood—two at the front and two at the back, held together with batten. Each semicircle is 1 in. wide. Mark them out on the marine plywood sheet and cut them out with a jigsaw, making the inside radius of the smaller semicircle 25 in. and the inside of the larger one 30 in. The best way to do this is to hammer a nail into the

plywood and tie a length of string to it. Then measure the radius that you want against the string and use it as a guide as you mark around your semicircle. Then cut out the first one of each size and draw around them to mark out the rest.

5 When they are all cut, sand down their edges and assemble them by setting a larger and a smaller semicircle out on a bench. Attach evenly spaced 2¾-in lengths of battens between them using copper tacks. Then tack two more semicircles on the top to sandwich the battens in place.

6 The diagonal lattice can be any height. The one in this project is 24 in., but its width must be the same as the distance between the outside beams of the end uprights. To measure this accurately, set out the uprights with the arches on their tops on level ground—as they would be on the wall. Once you have your measurements, cut and set out lengths of batten in a rectangle on the ground,

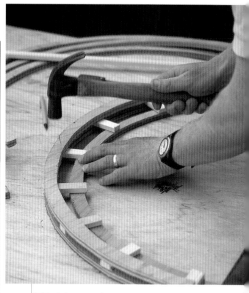

3 To make a plinth for the top of the upright, screw two rectangles together and screw them to the upright.

4 Mark out the semicircles on the marine plywood, and cut them with a jigsaw. Each arch is made up of four semicircles.

5 Tack battens between the semicircles, then place two more lengths of plywood on top to sandwich the battens in place.

then nail your diagonals to it. Keep the distance between the diagonals even with a spacer, and check that the outside rectangle remains square.

7 When both sets of diagonals are in place, turn the panel over so that the rectangular outer edge is uppermost, and position the arches side by side onto the top as shown. Check that the gaps between their ends and the outside of the trellis panel are the same, then mark around them with a pen and cut carefully along the lines with a jigsaw. When this job is done, cut away any lengths of diagonals that protrude beyond the outer rectangle with a jigsaw.

8 Make a plinth for the top of the diamond panel out of two rectangles of marine plywood screwed together, as in Step 3. As before, make the larger rectangle 1 in. wider than the smaller one. The lengths should be 3 in. and 2 in. longer than the diamond panel, which allows for an overhang. Paint the whole trellis with a protective wood stain—this is best done before fixing it to the wall, and if you have a lot to do, consider renting a paint sprayer.

Attaching the trellis to the wall is a two-person job. First, hold each piece in position and check that it is level, then drill a hole through it with a masonry bit, marking the brickwork below. Remove the trellis and drill into the bricks. Push a plastic screw anchor into the hole, put the trellis back, and fix with screws. Finally, screw the plinth onto the top of the diamond panel.

Planting

Plant climbers such as clematis (*Clematis*) and climbing roses (*Rosa*) at the feet of the columns so that they can grow up toward the arches. Clematis is a good choice, as its growth tends to be top-heavy, without much foliage below 5 ft., so they'll naturally fill the diamond lattice with flowers. Roses are easy to train and look fabulous when tied around the arches.

6 *Once you have calculated the measurements of your rectangle, set it out on the ground and nail your diagonals to it.*

7 *Next, lay the arches onto the diamond panel, mark around them, and then cut along the line with a jigsaw.*

8 *Having fixed your trellis to the wall using plastic screw anchors and screws, screw the plinth to the top of the diamond panel.*

split bamboo SCREEN

The crisp lines of a split bamboo screen can disguise all sorts of boundaries, from unattractive concrete posts and panels to boring wood fences. Bamboo screens need not be restricted to Japanese-style gardens either, because they can accentuate a tropical theme wherever large-leaved plants are grown. They work well in city gardens, where their strong vertical lines echo those of the surrounding urban jungle.

1 Broken, loose, or rotten posts in the existing fence will need to be replaced first. For concrete fence posts, use a masonry drill to make three holes in each—one at the top, one at the bottom, and one between the two—and insert plastic screw anchors.

2 Cut a set of uprights from rough-sawed wood that are 6 in. lower than the finished height of the screen, and screw them to the fence posts. Then measure and cut three rails for each upright and screw them in position with L-shaped brackets (to compensate for any leaning posts, measure and cut each rail individually). The framework isolates the screen from the fence panels, allowing them to be replaced or removed for access.

3 Unroll the bamboo and nail it to the framework using staples. To ensure that the top is level, sit the unrolled

MATERIALS

6¹/₂ × 16 ft. split bamboo screening

2 × 2 in. treated rough-sawed wood

¹/₂-in. staples

L-shaped brackets

1-in. screws

3-in screws

Plastic screw anchors (if the posts are concrete)

TOOLS

Masonry drill and bits

Screwdriver

Hammer

1 Using a powerful masonry drill, make three holes in the concrete fence posts and insert plastic screw anchors into the holes.

2 Having fixed rough-sawed wood uprights to the posts, cut three rails for each upright and screw them on.

Bamboo screens are manufactured in Vietnam and China, and since the late 1990s, new designs have become increasingly available. For an internal divide that looks good from both sides, heavy-duty, whole-cane screens, wired and strung between sturdy wood posts, are ideal. Screens with twiggy tops and side shoots have a thatchy, less formal look. The quality of bamboo screening can vary enormously, so check it carefully before purchasing.

3 Finally, staple the bamboo onto the framework, making sure it is level by resting its base on a wood plank.

screen on a wood plank before fixing with staples. This also keeps the bottom of the screen above the soil and helps extend its life.

Keeping up appearances for the neighbors
If you are raising the height of an external boundary with a screen, talk to your neighbors before starting, and keep in mind that the back of the screen and the woodwork that holds it in place will need to be disguised from their side. Do this either by fixing a trellis along the top of the fence or by covering the visible woodwork with a strip of screen. This leaves your neighbors with the existing fence topped with a neat screen coping.

Screen quality
Avoid screens that have frayed ends, slack wires, or uneven spaces. A good way of judging the quality is to pick up the roll. If it feels light, the chances are that the screen is of an inferior grade and will soon deteriorate in the garden.

hazelwood SCREEN

This undemanding, economical hazelwood garden screen makes a perfect boundary for a flower garden, allowing glimpses of the blooms within its borders as scented sweet peas (*Lathyrus odoratus*) clamber up its sides.

1 Push a series of uprights into the soil, choosing the straightest and thickest hazelwood rods for this job and leaving 2-ft. spaces between them. It's up to you whether the screen is straight, gently curved, or serpentine. The base of each rod should be pressed into the soil by at least 8 in. If the ground is too hard to do this by hand, make a hole with a fencing bar if you've got one, or open up a slit in the ground with a spade, press the hazelwood rod into the opening, and firm the soil around it. When all of the uprights are in, link them together with a horizontal rod tied to each one with twine at the height you want the screen.

2 The diagonals are pushed in next, at an angle of roughly 45°, with 12-in. spaces between them. Choose the longest lengths for the middle section of the screen, and use shorter, thinner rods for the corners. Because the

MATERIALS

Hazelwood rods

Twine

TOOLS

Fencing bar or spade

Pruning shears

1 Start by pushing a series of uprights at least 8 in. into the soil, using the straightest and thickest rods.

2 Next, push the diagonals into the soil, putting the longest lengths into the central section and leaving a 12-in. space between them.

KNOW YOUR MATERIALS

Hazelwood rods have long been used in gardens for plant supports. They are cheap to buy and easy to work with, so they are perfect for building temporary screens that can be dismantled and reassembled as the mood suits you. Each rod has a useful life of four or five years, after which time it becomes brittle and will need to be replaced. Many garden centers and lumberyards now supply hazelwood cut from local forests.

3 Tie the diagonals to the uprights, as well as where they cross the uprights. Twist their tops around the horizontals and tie them in.

diagonals at the top right and left of the screen are above soil level, and therefore can't be pushed into the ground, they need to be tied to the uprights with twine.

3 Tie the diagonals to the uprights and where they cross. Then twist their tops around the horizontal rods, holding them in place with twine. Alternately, you can bind them with a few lengths of willow, or simply cut them off just above the horizontal rods using pruning shears. Plant a row of sweet peas at the foot of the screen for scent, or use other annual climbers such as nasturtium (*Tropaeolum majus*), bright yellow canary creeper (*Tropaeolum peregrinum*), or electric blue morning glory (*Ipomoea tricolor*).

Alternative materials

For an Asian theme, use bamboo canes instead of the hazelwood rods, binding them together with lengths of tarred black string. String ties can be very ornamental, especially if the same knot is used throughout.

copper CLADDING

Copper is tremendously dynamic in a garden setting, due to the exotic blue-green patina it develops with time. It adds natural color without the risk of clashing, as can be the case with paint, and it imbues a small space with novelty and luxury.

1 Start by cladding the wall in ½-in. marine plywood to even out any irregularities in the brick- or plasterwork, and to create a smooth surface for gluing the copper. When cladding complicated walls like this alcove, make a template out of cardboard, making sure it fits the wall perfectly. Lay the template onto the marine plywood, draw around it, and cut it with a jigsaw. Fix the marine plywood to the wall by first propping it in position and drilling through every 27½ in. to mark the bricks beneath. Then remove it, drill the bricks, and insert plastic screw anchors. Prop the plywood back in place and hold it with screws.

2 Use the same cardboard template to mark the copper, using a marker pen to give a clear line. If there are any inaccuracies in the template, they'll be visible as gaps around the marine plywood on the wall, so as you mark

MATERIALS

Cardboard

½-in. marine plywood

Plastic screw anchors

Screws

Copper sheeting

Silicone glue or copper tacks

TOOLS

Jigsaw with sheet metal blade

Drill

Metal file

Rubber mallet, if using silicone
Glue or hammer, if using tacks

1 Make a template out of stiff cardboard and use it to cut out the marine plywood, which needs to be anchored to the wall.

2 Having used the template to mark the copper, cut the copper with a jigsaw, making sure the copper is well supported.

KNOW YOUR MATERIALS

To make your copper appear old
and weathered, burnish it in parts
with a gas torch from the kitchen,
the type chefs use to caramelize
crème brûlée. This treatment
creates dramatic dark blue clouds
against the vivid copper, colored
with rainbow shades, like gasoline
in a puddle. Stainless steel also
makes a good metal cladding.
Fix it onto marine plywood in
the same way as copper. Because
you can't cut it yourself, measure
the area first and buy it cut to
size. If you prefer the distressed,
seaside look of rusted metal, use
mild steel sheeting. Because of its
weight, bolt it directly to the wall.

the copper, adjust the line accordingly. Cut the copper
with a jigsaw fitted with a sheet metal blade. Copper is
surprisingly easy to cut. Keep the blade of the jigsaw close
to the side of the bench so that the copper is supported.
Once cut, use a metal file to smooth the edges.

3 The copper can be fixed with copper tacks or with
silicone glue. Because tacks are more obtrusive, it is
essential that they are hammered in symmetrical straight
lines or in deliberate swirls to keep them from detracting
from the sheet. To do this, mark their positions before
hammering them in. For a smooth finish, silicone glue is
best. This is available from building supply stores, along
with the gun needed to squeeze it from the tube. Apply
the glue in lines onto the marine plywood, taking
particular care to coat the corners. Then press the
copper sheet back onto it, tapping with a rubber mallet
to ensure good contact. Prop a length of wood against
the copper to hold it in place while the glue dries, which
takes between three and four hours.

3 *Squeeze silicone glue onto the marine plywood,*
then press the copper sheeting onto it. Tap it with
a rubber mallet to ensure good contact.

steel mesh SCREEN

For a modern take on trellises, steel mesh is the ideal alternative. Because it rusts, the orange complements the dark leaves of climbers like ivy (*Hedera*), making it a very handsome addition to your garden. Despite the fact that it rusts, the screen will last for years.

1 The supports for the mesh are made from boxed steel sections that are ¾ in. in diameter. Use a hacksaw to cut to the height of the screen plus 24 in. for fixing in the ground, and drill holes 24 in. apart right through the aboveground section. Give the belowground section a coat of rustproofing paint.

2 Mark the positions of the posts on the ground and dig a 12-in. hole for each. Then push the posts another 12 in. into the soil at the bottom of each hole, which holds them firm as you pour concrete (made from 1 part cement to 8 parts ballast) around their collars. (Use the fence post technique given on page 19 to level up the posts and ensure that they are the same height.) Smooth over the top of the collars with a trowel, so that any water runs away from the posts.

MATERIALS

4 x 6 ft. steel mesh with 8-in. squares

8-ft. lengths of 1-in. boxed steel

Rustproofing paint

Galvanized wire

Ballast

Cement

TOOLS

Masonry and bricklaying tools

Hacksaw

Drill

Pliers

1 Use a hacksaw to cut the boxed steel to length and drill holes in the aboveground section to support the mesh.

2 Dig holes for the uprights, pour concrete around them, and smooth over the top with a trowel.

The primary use for steel reinforcement mesh is for strengthening concrete footings and walls. It can be bought at any size from custom iron suppliers, who will build it to your specification. It is also available from building supply stores, although it will most likely be delivered in 10 x 25 ft. sheets; it will need to be cut down and possibly doubled up and wired together if the squares are larger than 6 in. Cut with a hacksaw or rent a bolt cutter to do the job.

For an extra touch of detail, moon gates and arched windows can be cut into the screen and given definition by braiding wire over the cut ends.

3 Put the steel mesh in position and tie it to the uprights with galvanized wire. Use pliers to twist and tighten the wire.

3 | Tie the panels to the posts with galvanized wire looped through the holes in the posts, tightening it by twisting with pliers. Plant ivy every 12 in. along the base of the screen; as it grows, train it to the metal. When it is established, prune with shears in early summer to encourage it to bush out, and feed with a general fertilizer.

Alternative materials

If the rusty look isn't your style, use stainless steel or aluminum screening with aluminum box section posts. These weather to a steely gray and never rust. Ironwork can be painted, but it needs to be rust free and painted with a primer first. Otherwise, the rust will appear after just a few months. For a more private screen with small diamond-shaped holes, use sheets of barbecue grate, which, as its name suggests, is more commonly used for cooking grills. Because the holes are small, barbecue grate looks particularly attractive at night when backlit with golden spotlights.

living boundaries

planning living boundaries

You cannot talk about boundaries without at least mentioning living ones. A garden is never complete without plants—it goes without saying that whether it's flowers growing in a dry stone wall, climbers rambling around a gate, or a hedge peeking over the top of a wooden fence, a boundary without plants is stark, cold, and never fully integrated.

Function and style Plants embellish garden boundaries by imparting a certain dynamism to otherwise static materials. It's a two-way street, of course, because the plants benefit from the microclimate created by the boundary and the support, while the boundary can claim more seasonality as the plants flower, change color in the fall, and spring into life early in the year.

Establishing Many people are more afraid of buying and growing plants than they are of do-it-yourself projects, but this is a misconception based on the belief that you have to grow the plants. The plants grow themselves! The thing to worry about is giving them the right spot to grow in and getting them established. The key is to improve the soil with store-bought compost, well-rotted manure, or homemade compost before planting. Then make sure plants are well watered, particularly during their first summer. If your problem is which plants to choose, check out plants that are thriving in neighbors' gardens and take advice from nearby nurseries or garden centers, because they will know which varieties do well in the local soil.

Design choices Walls—There are three ways in which plants can be combined with walls: climbers, cascading plants for the top of retaining walls, and growing plants within walls.

Low retaining walls make ideal falls for cascading plants, benefiting species that don't mind dry conditions and prefer to mound and tumble, rather than climb. Good subjects include grasses such as feather grass (*Stipa arundinacea*) and fox red curly sedge (*Carex buchananii*), shrubs like bearberry (*Cotoneaster dammeri*), and perennials like catnip (*Nepeta* 'Walkers Low') and many hardy geraniums

Living willow screen.

Hedge-topped fence.

Interwoven lime trees.

Formal hedge.

The look of a living boundary depends on the type of plants used and how they are maintained. Regularly clipped evergreens (top left) will become permanently neat boundaries, while training climbers across a trellis fence is an effective means of harnessing nature's inclination to riot (top right). For the ultimate trained boundary, you can't beat fruit trees with their main branches espaliered (wired horizontally) for a sculptural winter framework (above).

The branches of interwoven lime trees are grafted and twisted so that in time they grow together—as though they are holding hands.

(*Geranium maculatum*). Watering in the first year is essential for establishment. If you want plants to grow inside a wall, an irrigation hose should be installed during construction and plugged into the water supply regularly.

In ready-made walls, irrigation is often impossible to install. In such cases, the best way to plant them up is by sowing seed directly into soil-filled gaps. Of course, you can't put just anything in these gaps. You must choose plants that are naturally adapted to these tough conditions, such as alpines, or those that happily live on steep gravel beds in the wild. Good choices from seed include fleabane (*Erigeron karvinskianus*), Alpine toadflax (*Linaria alpina*), and thyme (*Thymus*). By sowing from seed, the plants are less likely to be shocked by the change in conditions than if they are transplanted from a pot. In time, they will produce seeds and colonize without your intervention. This is also a good technique for establishing plants like lady's mantle (*Alchemilla mollis*) at the base of a wall or between the gaps in paving.

Fences—There are two types of climbers: self-clinging ones and climbers that need support. Both can be combined with fences. It's often said that you shouldn't put self-clinging climbers onto a fence because of their weight, but this shouldn't be a concern if the fence is well-made. Self-clinging climbers, like Virginia creeper (*Parthenocissus quinquefolia*), Boston ivy (*Parthenocissus tricuspidata*), and ivy (*Hedera*), can look after themselves, but those with tendrils, such as clematis (*Clematis*), require a ladder of wires to help them climb. Using vine eyes to attach wires to the fence posts will allow space behind for climbers to grow and air to circulate. When planting, avoid the rain-shadow of the fence by leaving a space of 18 in. between the base and the planting hole. Tilt the rootball at a 45° angle toward the support to encourage it to climb in the direction you want.

Trellises—Because a trellis is flimsier, keep stems from growing behind the beams, as they can push the trellis out of shape as they grow. Train the stems onto the support by tying them to the front with soft twine.

Hedges—Hedges are cheaper and usually blend in more with their surroundings than a new hard structure, but they take longer to reach a good height. Combine the hedge with a formal iron railing fence or a cottage garden picket. A clever combination is a yew (*Taxus*) clipped into the back of a privacy fence, so that the internal screen is a living hedge, while the outside world sees a solid wood boundary.

All living boundaries bring seasonality to a garden, but beech (Fagus) and hornbeam (Carpinus) are particularly dynamic—greening up in spring and retaining russet color through fall and the worst of the winter. Hornbeam takes training particularly well (above left), and its main branches can be clipped into giant walls, like the beech (above right).

Trellis on a panelled fence.

Half-round peeled posts.

Interwoven hedge with ash tree.

A frost-covered beech hedge.

willow WALL

Earth and willow wands may not seem like a promising combination for a wall, but together they make a long-lasting, strong boundary. If the wall is also planted with wildflowers and grasses, its sides will flower and color with the changing seasons.

1 Mark the footing of the wall on the ground with paint, spacing the two sides of the wall 24 in. apart and connecting their ends with a gentle curve. For strength, make the sides serpentine. Then use shears to cut the base of the thicker willow into 3-ft. lengths to make the uprights, measuring at least ³/₄ in. in diameter at their thinnest end. Push the uprights into the ground 10–12 in. apart; angle the tops of the two sides together to give the sides an A-shaped profile. Having an uneven number of uprights makes weaving easier, so add an extra one, adjusting the spacing of its neighbors to make it fit. Hammer them in firmly with a wooden mallet or beetle.

2 Using single lengths of the thinner willow, weave in and out of the uprights about halfway up their sides. As you reach the end of each length, tuck it inside of the wall. Introduce another willow length, matching the thick end

MATERIALS

Bundles of willow 1–2 in.
in diameter for the uprights

Bundles of graded willow ¹/₂ in.
in diameter for the sides

Irrigation pipe

Topsoil

Turf

TOOLS

Carpentry tools

Pruning shears

Mallet or beetle

1 Having cut the lengths for the uprights, push them into the ground, spacing them 10–12 in. apart.

2 Weave single lengths of willow in and out of the uprights halfway up their sides, and tuck the end of each length inside the wall.

KNOW YOUR MATERIALS

Willow is a fabulous building material, which is strong, malleable, and easy to work with. It is available from specialty growers who supply bundles of willow by mail order. To save money, look through the phone book for screen makers, thatchers, or nature reserves who may point you to a cheaper local source. The time to buy is in the dormant season when the willow is cut, because summer stocks run out quickly.

The willow used for this project is the fresh green common osier (*Salix viminalis*). Also available are brightly colored willows, such as the orange *S. alba* 'Britzensis' and the black *S. daphnoides* 'Aglaia,' which both add striking detail to new structures.

of one to the thin end of the other until you've gone around the structure twice. If you have an odd number of uprights, the second layer of willow will alternate with the first, and each upright will be firmly bound inside and out. Check your weave against the photograph, and working around the wall, push the willow down until it is in contact with the ground.

3 The first two layers of willow rods hold the uprights steady while you weave in the remainder. Take up to four or five lengths at a time and tap them down so that their thick ends are together, then weave them in and out of the uprights. As before, introduce another handful when the first comes to its end. Work around the wall, making sure that each course alternates with the one below.

4 To use the willow efficiently, spread the rods in each handful out flat so that they have the widest spread. Don't worry about any small gaps, as these will be filled by grasses and flowers once the wall is established.

When the sides of the wall reach half their finished height, fill between them with soil, firming it into the corners with the soles of your feet (it's much easier to do this as you go along, rather than after the sides are complete).

5 Weave up to the finished height of between $27^{1}/_{2}$ in. and 36 in., filling with soil and firming as you go, taking care to maintain the wall's A-shaped profile. If the sides start to splay, tie vertically across the wall with nylon rope or thick string to hold them together. Then cut the tops of the uprights level and trim off any straggly tops or protruding ends using a pair of pruning shears.

6 Cut the irrigation pipe to the length of the wall, tie a knot in one end, and attach a hose adaptor to the other. Lay the pipe on top of the wall and feed the end with the hose adaptor through the side in an inconspicuous place.

3 Take four or five lengths at a time and weave them through the uprights, ensuring that each course alternates with the one below.

4 Once the sides of the wall have reached half their height, fill between them with soil, firming it in by tamping down with your feet.

5 Having weaved up to the finished height and filled with soil, tidy up the wall by cutting off protruding ends with pruning shears.

7 | Next cover the hose with more soil, doming it up 4–6 in. over the height of the sides to fill any gaps if the soil inside the wall settles. Then lay turf along the top of the wall or plant with a mixture of English primroses (*Primula vulgaris*), Lady's mantle (*Alchemilla*), and geraniums (*Geranium*).

8 | To fill the pockets between each layer of willow, sow a mixture of wildflower seeds, such as ox-eye daisies (*Chrysanthemum leucanthemum*) and foxgloves (*Digitalis*). In the fall, plant bluebells (*Campanula rotundifolia*) and daffodils (*Narcissus*) to flower the following spring. Alternately, use herbaceous plants—in this project variegated hosta (*Hosta*) and lemon balm (*Melissa officinalis*) sprouted from the sides after smuggling themselves into the wall as roots mixed with the topsoil. They are now thriving in their new lofty position.

Using and caring for willow

A willow wall works both as an internal divide and around a perimeter. It looks good in any location, whether urban or rural. In a country setting, its soft, flowery sides blend perfectly with its surroundings, adding loads of cottage garden charm. In a contemporary garden, when mixed in with man-made materials such as glass and metal, the naturalness and country craft of the wall become more apparent.

Willow has a dogged ability to survive, even after the harshest treatment. So much so that the cut branches will happily sprout new leaves, even after being hammered into the ground. This tenacity makes willow ideal for soil-filled walls, because the stems quickly regrow, binding the sides together with their roots. To keep it from taking over and squeezing out the wildflowers, use shears to prune back the fresh stems that appear throughout the summer. Connect a hose to the irrigation pipe in periods of drought, switching it on for an hour at a time to ensure all the soil inside the wall gets a good soak.

6 *Lay irrigation pipe along the length of the wall, tying up one end and feeding the end with a hose adaptor discreetly through the side.*

7 *Having covered the hose with soil domed up above the height of the sides, lay turf along the top.*

8 *Finally, fill the pockets between each layer of willow rods with a mixture of wildflower seeds, such as foxgloves.*

hedge WINDOW

A circular window will instantly give hedges character, color, and charm. In gardens made somber by shady, tall hedges, a window will instantly brighten up their face and lift the shadow they cast.

1 The window frame is supported in the hedge on an H-shaped wood mount, which consists of a crosspiece that is cut to the width of the window frame and two uprights cut to 4 in. above the height you want for the center of the window. Mark the position of the crosspiece by laying the uprights on level ground and setting the window between them with its center 4 in. below their tops. Fix the crosspiece below the window using L-shaped brackets and wood screws.

2 The feet of the mount are held in the hedge with fence spikes, which can be hammered into the line of the hedge without causing excessive root disturbance. Make sure that the fence spikes are spaced to the same width as the mount (if the trunks of the hedge plants correspond with the spikes, position them just in front of the trees). Use a fence spike driving tool to protect their

MATERIALS

3-in. fence spikes

3-in. posts

Circular window

4-in. screws

Four L-shaped brackets

Dark wood stain for posts

Glass paint or stained glass (optional)

TOOLS

Masonry and bricklaying tools

Crosscut saw

Drill and pilot bit

Fence spike driving tool

1 Make an H-shaped mount for the window using 3-in. fence posts fixed together with L-shaped brackets.

2 Hammer the two fence spikes into the line of the hedge. Space the spikes to the width of the mount.

KNOW YOUR MATERIALS

The most economical way to buy a circular window is from a salvage yard. The condition can be variable, so check over the frame to make sure that the woodwork is sound. Don't worry if the glass is broken, because glass is cheaper and easier to replace than damaged beams or rotten wood. Clean up the glass and replace any cracked sections, and then give the frame a coat of wood preservative to protect it from the weather.

tops as you hammer. In hedges with dense foliage, it is easier to construct the mount in situ by tapping the uprights into the fence spikes and then attaching the crosspiece in the hedge. To help disguise the wood, paint it with a black or dark brown wood stain.

3 Rest the window onto the crosspiece, secure it by pilot-drilling angled holes through the face of the window frame into the uprights, and fix it with 4-in. screws.

Tie branches that block the window back with string, and hide the mount by pulling foliage in front of it. Use shears to prune any branches that obscure the glass and are too big to tie back. After installing the window, the hedge will need a few months to grow around it completely. To encourage this process, water and feed during the growing season, clipping when necessary.

3 Secure the window onto the crosspiece by pilot-drilling angled holes through the window frame into the uprights.